fanboys and overdogs
the language report

fanboys and overdogs
the language report

SUSIE DENT

OXFORD
UNIVERSITY PRESS

OXFORD

UNIVERSITY PRESS

Great Clarendon Street, Oxford OX2 6DP

Oxford University Press is a department of the University of Oxford.
It furthers the University's objective of excellence in research, scholarship,
and education by publishing worldwide in

Oxford New York

Auckland Cape Town Dar es Salaam Hong Kong Karachi
Kuala Lumpur Madrid Melbourne Mexico City Nairobi
New Delhi Shanghai Taipei Toronto

With offices in

Argentina Austria Brazil Chile Czech Republic France Greece
Guatemala Hungary Italy Japan Poland Portugal Singapore
South Korea Switzerland Thailand Turkey Ukraine Vietnam

Oxford is a registered trademark of Oxford University Press
in the UK and in certain other countries

Published in the United States
by Oxford University Press Inc., New York

British Library Cataloguing in Publication Data
Data available

Library of Congress Cataloging in Publication Data
Data available

Typeset by Paul Saunders
Printed in Great Britain
by Clays Ltd, Bungay, Suffolk

ISBN 0-19-280676-9
ISBN 978-0-19-280676-5

1

In memory of Richard Whiteley,
for his laughter and his love of words

Acknowledgements

To put just one name on the title page of this third *language report* feels very fraudulent. A very large number of people contributed to it—some unwittingly. Language holds such strong fascination that almost every conversation I had (or heard) about the subject armed me with new material or ideas. I couldn't begin to thank everyone who contributed in that way, but it made the writing of the book much easier, and much more fun.

Some of those conversations were, of course, with people who helped me in a bigger way by contributing whole series of examples and ideas on particular topics. Many of them have contributed to previous *language reports*, and the ongoing survey of language trends owes much to their vigilance and insight. Andrew Ball provided intriguing material on catchphrases and headlines (and a lot else), Jane McCauley gave a fascinating report on the ongoing work on the *Oxford English Dictionary*, and her colleague Graeme Diamond shared his expertise for the *Word a Year* selection. The latter would have been almost impossible without the technical expertise and editorial insight of James McCracken.

The section on slang owes its vibrancy and detail to Jonathon Green, to whom I am extremely grateful. Martin Cutts and the Plain Language Commission suggested some excellent examples of jargon at its worst. Orin Hargraves provided many gems from the US: he and Erin McKean were once again reassuring transatlantic correspondents throughout. Gijs Elsen and Thierry Morel proved perfect sounding boards for new ideas, and contributed many of their own, as did Darren Jordon, who also gave me some wonderful examples of Jamaican patois.

Angus Stevenson was again an excellent source of advice on our changing grammar and usage; the charting of music vocabulary is also entirely thanks to him. Catherine Soanes was of enormous help throughout the project, tirelessly sending in new examples of language change together with her own valuable judgements on it, and always responding immediately to a daily barrage of email questions. I also owe huge thanks to my commissioning editor, Judy Pearsall, both for her continuing faith in the project and for reading the entire typescript when she should have been convalescing.

Rachel De Wachter, Karen Vining, Carol Alexander, Nick Clarke, John Taylor, Helen Liebeck, and Paul Saunders were all part of a top editorial and production team.

Final thanks are due to Elizabeth Knowles, who once again proved the best adviser and helpmate I could hope for. And to Rebecca Gowers, for her daily gems and for her suggestions for new areas to tackle. To their support and original thinking the book owes much.

Susie Dent, 2005

Notes on trademarks and proprietary status

Contents

Introduction

The language report cannot hope to be comprehensive. Any attempt to capture all notable shifts in the English language for 2005, across untold classes of speakers and writers, is impossible. Even in the time that lapses between assembling the report and getting it out in print, language will have moved on.

Yet there is a strong argument for monitoring the shifting language scene, for attempting to record its mutations, and for probing the reasons for them. One aim of all three language reports, 2003-2005, has been to prove the value of putting down markers, not least to provide clues for the future as to what English looked like from the inside in the year under review. The reports are also, of course, designed to give readers in the present an overview of language change spanning many areas, going beyond any individual new words that enjoy a high profile. It attempts to note patterns where they exist, and to ponder the lack of them where they appear not to.

Most importantly, it is the very mutability of English that makes it so interesting, exciting, and challenging, and that arouses such passion in its speakers. The 2005 report feels particularly worthwhile given that English is at present far more frequently noted for its state of decline than its vitality. Yet that vitality can surely hardly be doubted. However brief the life of some of the neologisms included here—one could take an each-way bet, for example, on whether 'bromance' or 'clicktrance' will survive much beyond these pages—their exuberance suggests that our enjoyment of language, and the creativity to which this gives rise, is far from diminishing. A hundred years ago, 'slummocker', 'pomato' and 'smog' were among the many new terms gaining a foothold. Today's 'bluesnarfing', 'memail' and 'boomburbs' suggest no let-up in linguistic relish.

For some, that creativity is at the expense of linguistic correctness, and goes hand in hand with—to use that now stock phrase—a dumbing down. Complaints about the state of English tend to focus on two areas: bad usage, and bad language. Laments continue over a perceived decline in standards, seen often as a consequence of modern technology and the pull it exerts towards improper speed. The debate about the effects of the globalization of English, and the extraordinary spread of its use through the Internet, rumbles on.

The distinction between organic language evolution on the one hand, and incorrect usage on the other, is notoriously a blurred one. Tension between the two, however, is not new: every age has had its linguistic bugbears, and some distinctly linger. Henry Fowler, in his *Modern English Usage* (1926), rued the use of 'disinterested' for 'uninterested'. Rising a century later, his successors have been swift to point out Tony Blair's misuse of the same term in his soundbite description of an apathetic electorate: one which is, 'not disinterested, but disempowered'.

As for bad language: in 1965, the journalist John Cohen observed that 'the man who first abused his fellows with swear-words, instead of bashing their brains out with a club, should be counted among those who laid the foundations of civilization.' His words came after the now infamous episode in which the critic Kenneth Tynan used the word 'fuck' live on national TV. Fifty years on, the public response to the profanity of *Jerry Springer, The Opera*, and the continuing censorship within US broadcasting, suggests that linguistic taboos still hold considerable power.

A report such as this one cannot hope to give a definitive diagnosis of the health of our language, nor a prognosis of its future. Given that the text is operating within a tight time-frame, it may well raise more questions than it endeavours to answer. If, however, this book provokes argument, and causes its readers to think of unmentioned examples, or of interesting counter-examples, then it has already served a purpose. English may be under assault from globalization and from new media, but this same assault opens up opportunities for self-renewal. There has never been a finite golden age in our language's history, nor a monolithic, unified

English. Splendid diversity has been a constant over the course of its 1,500 year history. If variation has never been as great as it is now, this is surely more likely to stretch our language than diminish it. We can only guess at where English is heading; for the moment, though, there is plenty to marvel at. The primary aim of the 2005 language report is to highlight some of the many reasons to celebrate.

Susie Dent, 2005

The Language of Events | **1**

The Somme is like the Holocaust. It revealed things about mankind that we cannot come to terms with and cannot forget. It can never become the past.
Pat Barker, English novelist, on winning the 1995 Booker Prize for *The Ghost Road*.

Her pout, always volcanic, seems almost nuclear. It's Chernobyl-esque.
Tanya Gold writing in *The Guardian* about the actress Scarlett Johansson.

Early in 2005, sixty years after Auschwitz was liberated, the London mayor Ken Livingstone likened a Jewish journalist to a 'concentration camp guard'. The outrage and shock which followed revealed the residual strength of the term **concentration camp** and its immediate evocation of the Holocaust. The word **Holocaust** itself became the recognized symbol of the atrocities of the German Nazi regime in the Second World War, its capital letter emphasizing its specificity.

In fact, both terms were in existence long before the events with which they are now inextricably linked. Yet their previous history has been overshadowed. Just as quotations distil a historical situation or event, so individual words and phrases may come to capture a single moment or period in history, no matter how long and general a currency those words might have had before.

The concept of the 'concentration camp', designed originally for the internment of civilians, was instituted by Lord Kitchener during the Boer War of 1899–1902 and was controversial even at the time. The *Oxford*

English Dictionary's first citation for the term comes from the Hansard record of a debate in the British Parliament in 1901, where discussion was held of 'the policy of placing the women and children confined in the concentration camps in South Africa, whose husbands and fathers are in the field, on reduced rations'.

The term 'holocaust' dates back in English to the thirteenth century, when it denoted 'a sacrifice wholly consumed by fire; a whole burnt offering'. In the sixteenth century the word had come to mean 'a sacrifice on a large scale'; by the seventeenth Milton was using the term, in *Samson Agonistes*, to mean the complete consumption by fire of a great number of people. For three hundred years after that, 'holocaust' was readily used to denote slaughter on a large scale. Following the mass murders perpetrated by the Nazi regime, it was historians who gave the term a definite article and capital letter, seeking the same kind of uniqueness that the Nazis themselves had found in *Die Endlösung*, or 'the final solution'. For most, 'the Holocaust' acquired the single meaning of the mass human destruction of that time. Some people consider the term inadequate: in 1967 the journal *Judaism* noted: 'But there have been other holocausts, and they were nothing like this. In such a linguistic perplexity Jews... turn to Hebrew... Thus we try the word *sho'ah*.' Like 'Holocaust', **Shoah**, the literal meaning of which in modern Hebrew is 'catastrophe', has acquired a capital letter in its reference to a specific historical event.

Many more of those words which carry indelible associations of the past are war- or death-related, perhaps inevitably. From **the trenches** of the First World War, and **the Troubles** of Northern Ireland, to the very recent **shock and awe** strategy of the Americans in Iraq, each conflict has acquired its own terminology. However evocative, the results are not always straightforward. The Second World War saw **swastika** transformed from a symbol of fortune into an emblem of evil. The term, derived from the Sanskrit *svastika* meaning well-being or luck, is packed with associations of its Nazi adaptation, in spite of continuing use as a positive religious symbol in Hindu and Buddhist cultures where it has held a benign significance for centuries. The degree of protest which followed Prince Harry's choice of a swastika'd armband for a fancy dress party revealed that neither the symbol nor its name has lost the power to shock.

Political and diplomatic strategies are often given labels, many of which become more or less official. To hear **the road map** today is to instantly understand the allusion to 'the road map to peace', the initiative to introduce peace between the Israelis and Palestinians, just as **the peace process** became instant shorthand for the one for Northern Ireland. Looking further back, **appeasement** was a term freely used in political contexts in the twentieth century; since 1938 however it has most often been used (disparagingly) in reference to the attempts at conciliation by concession made by the British Prime Minister Neville Chamberlain before the outbreak of war with Germany in 1939. By extension the term now denotes any such policy of pacification by concession to an enemy. Another unpopular term, **subsidiarity**, was one of the buzzwords of the European Parliament in the 1980s. It was defined to mean that the European Community's activities should be limited to those which are better performed in common than by member states individually. For politicians it seemed to have the added advantage that no one really knew what it meant.

When a word adheres itself to a single event it does not, however, become frozen in time or run counter to the momentum of language and its constant process of evolution. Just as only the smallest percentage of new words are entirely new creations—the vast majority are reworkings of existing words or parts of them—so the language of events can be reused or adapted to meet new circumstances. In this case, the intention is almost always to recall the past, to capture previous associations by adapting previous (and crucially, remembered) formulations. In the run-up to the offensive on Iraq, Tony Blair described his eleventh-hour attempts to secure a resolution from the UN Security Council as **mobile phone diplomacy**, a phrase which he knew carried echoes of the former British Foreign Secretary Lord Carrington's reference to **megaphone diplomacy** as well as of Henry Kissinger's **shuttle diplomacy** as the only way to negotiate with the Soviet Union.

One of the most memorable phrases of 1992 was **annus horribilis**, chosen by the Queen in her Christmas broadcast to describe a year of difficulty for the Royal Family including the fire at Windsor Castle. The phrase, which reverses the 'annus mirabilis' found in fifteenth-century predictions by astronomers and astrologers, has been reused on many occasions since, each of them making a tacit nod to the Queen. *The Boston Herald* described Britney Spears's '55-hour Vegas marriage' to a childhood chum as an appropriate end to 'an **annus trashus** for the former Mouseketeer'.

Echoes from the past are made more explicit when a linguistic formula is set and followed. That established by Watergate has proved one of the most popular, with **-gate** becoming the suffix of choice when any scandal, political or otherwise, threatens to have serious consequences for its participants. 2005's successors to **Cheriegate**, **Camillagate**, and **Zippergate** (referring to the alleged behaviour of Bill Clinton, who saw **Monicagate** govern the headlines soon after), were **Rooneygate** (after footballer Wayne Rooney was said to have paid for the services of a prostitute), and **Nannygate** (thanks to the then Home Secretary David Blunkett who was said to have expedited the granting of a visa to his lover's nanny). Of course, some of these coinages will be short-lived but the existance of '-gate' as a productive controlling element is now established.

Momentous events form new linguistic connections. The date of **September 11**, or **9/11**, is now immediate shorthand both for the events of that day in 2001 and for its aftermath. As well as its mainstream use as a noun, it is used attributively as an adjective ('September 11th backlash', '9/11 victims'), and even as a verb ('all of us, wherever we were, were 9/11ed'), the date will never regain its neutrality. Similarly **ground zero**, used until 9/11 to denote the part of the ground situated immediately under an exploding bomb and in particular reference to Hiroshima, as now used, denotes the site where New York's Twin Towers stood.

Hiroshima is a further example of a single word, in this case a name, which sums up an event and which needs no further clarification. Topographical labels for historical events are often among the most potent. **Suez**, **Dresden**, **the Somme**, **Passchendaele**, **Jonestown**, **Chernobyl**, **Dunblane**, **Lockerbie**, **Columbine**: each of these place names is a strong reminder of a particular event.

A magnificent war of words

2005 marked the fortieth anniversary of Winston Churchill's death. Churchill was one of the notable examples in recent history of people who use language in such an individual way that they forge a strong link between circumstance and vocabulary. His influence on language goes beyond the stock of famous sayings which are so frequently replayed. While not the originator of the **iron curtain**, which was used to mean an impenetrable barrier as early as 1819, Churchill is credited by the *OED* for giving it the specific sense of a barrier to the passage of information between the Soviet Union and the Western Allies. His phrase **summit meeting** also passed quickly into everyday use.

Churchill's language was powerfully emotive at a time when a strength of conviction was clearly needed. In a study of the PM's speeches, the writer David Cannadine notes that he 'used language as his most powerful weapon when his most frequent complaint was that the armoury was otherwise empty'. When asked, some years after the conflict, to comment on his pivotal role in the Second World War, the man known as the British bulldog replied in typically robust mode: **The nation had the lion's heart, I had the luck to give the roar**.

In February 2005, on the eve of the ban on hunting with hounds in Britain, one hunt master borrowed a Churchillian catchphrase to summarize his determination to continue with his chosen pursuit, offering simply: **I intend to keep buggering on**.

2004 ended with a striking example of the appropriation of a word by an event. The Asian **tsunami** forced a previously little-known word into the everyday vocabulary of millions. In the following months the tragedy was called simply 'the tsunami', and frequently 'The Tsunami', and no further elaboration was needed. Until the disaster this Japanese word, meaning harbour (*tsu*) wave (*nami*), was largely confined to the vocabulary of seismologists and geography students. Following the event not only did laypeople know the technical meaning of the word, but 'tsunami' started appearing in figurative uses to describe a sudden influx, or deluge, of something. More serious consequences followed the punning of the sports commentator Rodney Marsh when he conflated 'tsunami' with the 'Toon Army', the term for fans of Newcastle United. He was fired from his radio job as a result.

All these instances suggest that words can be powerful distillations of their times. Individual quotations, and particular words and phrases, hold on to their associations with history long after new events and characters have taken over.

Bubbling Under:
The Words of the Moment

2

Finding a name for something is a way of conjuring its existence, of making it possible for people to see a pattern where they didn't see anything before.
American writer and editor Howard Rheingold.

Every year, thousands of new words, meanings, and phrases come into the English language. Of these, the majority are picked up by Oxford's worldwide monitoring programme and tracked for signs of endurance, since any new word added to a dictionary must necessarily show strong signs of survival. Far from occupying a state of limbo, those words under observation for their staying power are continuously being refined or modified as they pass from user to user. To borrow a term used of singles in the music charts, they are 'bubbling under' the surface. Only time will tell as to whether they will gain sufficient exposure to enter the dictionary.

New words can come from anywhere, but most relate clearly to their cultural or historical context. 'A community,' the American linguist John Algeo has written, 'is known by the language it keeps.' The coinages that surface in any given year provide a series of cultural snapshots which together form an evocative, but not necessarily accurate picture of the prevailing culture. They chronicle history in the same way as a quotation from an event can do, even if some need more unpacking than others.

The following is a selection of some of the most recent and interesting words and phrases to be catching the lexicographer's eye. They represent undomesticated language: what Paul McFedries, editor of the website

Wordspy, calls the 'wild, untrammelled neologisms' which come to occupy new linguistic territory.

crackberry

crackberry: a BlackBerry hand-held device which is used obsessively. The term, which can also denote an obsessive user of a BlackBerry device, is a reference to the computer's addictive quality, and plays on 'crack' meaning 'cocaine'.

BlackBerries are nicknamed CrackBerries for a reason. Just ask U.S. Rep. Peter Deutsch, who checked his BlackBerry twice during a live televised debate against other candidates for a Senate seat.

NetworkWorldFusion, August 2004.

fugly

fugly: a euphemism formed by blending 'fucking ugly' or 'fuck-ugly', and used as a verb, an adjective, and a noun. The term, which dates back to the 1980s (*fug* has been an alternative for *fuck* for longer), is a new buzzword in fashion circles and is also used in hundreds of blogs and websites. It is used, for example, to express shock or horror at a celebrity's perceived fashion faux pas, while 'fugliness' is also seen as a deliberately choreographed ugliness, as in the wearing of 'Ugg' boots.

I must be feeling rather metrosexual today—I think this site, Go Fug Yourself, which catches stars looking at their worst, is great. In an age of obsession and airbrush, it's nice to see these folks looking, so, well, fugly.

Extract from a personal blog, December 2004.

gene editing

gene editing: a potentially revolutionary technique developed by scientists in California, whereby genes in the human body can be 'rewritten' to correct mutations which cause such genetic diseases as sickle cell anaemia. Some commentators fear the abuse of gene editing by parents who wish to alter the physical characteristics of their children for more superficial reasons.

Gene editing exploits the body's natural ability to repair broken strands of DNA. Clinical trials of its ability to stop the HIV virus infecting immune system cells will start in humans next year.

The Guardian, April 2005.

machosexual

machosexual: a 'blokeish' man who cares little for his appearance and whose attitude towards style is the opposite of the 'metrosexual'.

A machosexual is little different from a retrosexual: a man who spends as little time and money on his appearance as possible.

Machosexuals are resistant to fashion and hearken to the call of adventure with the same passion that metrosexuals adore grooming products.

Robert Young Pelton in *The Observer*, March 2005.

golden rice

golden rice: a new strain of genetically modified rice which produces large amounts of beta-carotene, converted in the body to vitamin A. The rice, developed by British scientists, has been designed to improve the sight of children in the Third World.

Infiltrating words

The rise of Internet and hi-tech fraud is reflected in new terminology which is often as ingenious as the measures produced to counteract it.

slurpware: the term used for the large collection of computer tools needed to carry out web-based financial fraud. The use of *slurping up* to refer to the gathering of sensitive data is more established.

'Slurpware' requires a community of trusted users, phishing mail, password slurping malware, and sponsorship of the Russian mafia.

Jay Heiser, a vice president and research director at Gartner Inc, reporting in *Business Day*, South Africa, February 2005.

botnet: a collection of software 'robots' which run autonomously under a common control infrastructure, and the weapon of choice for 'cybergangs' who commit fraud. Such criminals propagate viruses or spyware which are downloaded onto unprotected computers. At a designated time, the infected computers bombard a chosen target with junk data until it eventually collapses.

Botnets are marauders waiting at the edge of every network for the one vulnerable machine that will become their key through enterprise fortifications.

searchsecurity.com, March 2005.

sniffing (a more familiar term is **keylogging**): the practice of recording every keystroke a computer user makes by secretly installing a special program. The results are used to gain access to a user's password and other private details in order to commit 'cyber-heists'.

spear phishing: a highly targeted form of 'phishing', the fraudulent practice of sending emails from an apparently trusted source requesting personal information such as passwords. Unlike standard phishing, in which emails are sent to a general population via widespread spam emails, spear phishers target just one organization. The compound keeps alive the original metaphor of 'fishing'.

Some of the sneakiest 'spear phishing' scams target eBay customers, mainly because buyers and sellers are accustomed to receiving e-mails prompting them to take certain actions at specific times.

Washington Post, November 2004.

spit

spit: the voicemail equivalent of spam (unsolicited commercial email) which is sent via Internet telephony. One company has introduced a 'spitfilter' and predicts the advent of 'spitbots' to counter such messages. Further new terms in this vein are **spim**, unwanted advertising sent via instant messaging systems, and **skam**, a play on 'spam' and the name of the Internet telephony company Skype, denoting the sending of unsolicited messages from individuals outside a user's contact list.

erotourism

erotourism: a form of 'experimental tourism', whereby a couple travel to the same destination but go separately with the aim of finding each other. The purpose of erotourism is to rekindle romance in a relationship.

back, sack, and crack

back, sack, and crack: a waxing procedure in which a man's body hair is removed from his back, genitals, and between his buttocks. An alternative term which has also surfaced is **boyzilian**, a play on a woman's **Brazilian** wax.

Man, I feel like a woman. I've had my eyebrows plucked and combed into a 'now brow'. . . . shortly after checking into Loews, you find yourself in the Ocean Spa with a beautician called Adrianne, who offers you a BCS—a 'back, sack and crack' wax— and only takes no for an answer when you agree to let her pluck your eyebrows.

John Arlidge in *The Observer*, March 2005.

memail

memail: an email sent purely to gain attention. The term may be related to the search engine Google's personalized email service MeMail.

Sent to large numbers of correspondents using the reply-all button, memails contain no substance. Their sole function is to draw attention to the sender, using the fewest words possible. Recently received examples include 'that's just great', 'good news', 'fantastic', or just plain 'yup'. What can be done?

Vassili Papastavrou, letters page of *The Guardian*, April 2005.

blood spinning

blood spinning: a method used to treat sports injuries, in which platelets are removed from a blood sample taken from an injured player or athlete, and then re-injected back into the patient. The therapy is believed by some to speed up healing. The use of the technique by the British football club Chelsea came under investigation by the World Anti-Doping Agency in 2005.

Botaxes

Botaxes (or vanity taxes): taxes on plastic surgery procedures, including Botox injections.

Botaxes? They send exactly the wrong message. We should be trying to look better, not worse. If we get any uglier, we're in danger of scaring off all those foreign tourism dollars. What's next? A $10 surcharge with each purchase of Spanx Power Panties?

Chicago Sun-Times, 2005.

overdog

overdog: another term for 'top dog', or a person who is successful and dominant in their field (the opposite of an underdog). The first citation of the word in the *Oxford English Dictionary* refers to an actual dog, while the figurative sense came into play in 1938. In the 2000s it is used to mean someone who has a distinct advantage over someone else.

Fanatical fandom

An enduring term of the 1990s and 2000s is **fanboy**, a word which is gaining currency outside the fairly narrow circle in which it has been used up till now. A fanboy is a passionate male enthusiast of a hobby within so-called 'geek' culture, including comic books and video, computer, adventure, and fantasy games. The term seems to have originated in comic book circles where it denoted somebody who hid their insecurities behind their obsession. It tends to be used disparagingly, particularly by less fanatical participants in the same hobby.

The stereotypical fanboy is one who cares little for his appearance and who otherwise contributes little to the world around him, although more recently the term has been embraced by groups of gamers who are evangelical about their hobby and who actively promote it to others. The Comic Book Guy on the US cartoon show *The Simpsons* is seen as typical of the fanboy.

The female equivalent of the fanboy is a **fangirl**.

third

third: a long-stemmed beer glass carrying a third of a pint, plans for which were launched in 2005 by the British Beer and Pub Association as part of a campaign to present beer to women as an alternative to wine. The Association apparently supposes that women might find traditional half or full pint glasses too heavy. A *Times* article discussing the idea was headed 'Does my beer look big in this?'

...a spokesman explained the benefits, claiming that women would be able to drink their 'thirds' without 'spilling it all over their shoes'. Obviously we would like to extend the warm hand of gratitude to the BBPA for thinking of our kitten heels.

Women's page of *The Guardian*, March 2005.

Ingerland

Ingerland: This represents the England football team as known by its supporters, and so is used as a respelling of the pronunciation of England by fans when they chant it at matches. The term, which is often used by journalists to encapsulate the aggressive behaviour of some English football fans, is also used more generally for its connotation of a highly patriotic (or even racist) perception of English national identity.

security mom

security mom: a mother whose political agenda is seen to consist of one overriding issue: the security of her family. The term is an extension of 'soccer mom' and has grown out of the growing fear of terrorism since 9/11. 'Security moms' are said to make up 14% of the US electorate. The British equivalent **security mum** was mooted as a rising political force in the 2005 general election (called among other things the **schoolgate election**).

I am what this year's election pollsters call a 'security mom'. I'm married with two young children. I own a gun. And I vote. Nothing matters more to me right now than the safety of my home and the survival of my homeland.

Michelle Malkin in *USA Today*, July 2004.

To coin a phrase

Some of the idioms of the moment:

to step away from the — : to move away from something; to avoid something. The phrase began as part of police language in 'step away from the gun', popularized by TV police shows. It is now used humorously and metaphorically to mean to distance oneself from anything in any situation. 'Drop the mouse and step away from the pc' is the heading of one 2005 article on *msn.com* discussing 'computer rage'.

to throw it down: to put on a great performance, thereby soundly defeating the competition. The figurative use is an extension of a baseball term used in reference to slam-dunking a basket. A **throwdown** is a rap competition.

come-to-Jesus: this phrase, found largely in business contexts, denotes a summit called to stop something which has gone terribly wrong or to change dramatically the course of something in progress. 'Come to Jesus' has long been the refrain of evangelical Christian revival meetings, in which one would be adjured to do this after an inspiring sermon. This use goes back to at least the nineteenth century.

When the new Army colonel arrived to replace Maj G, he quickly sensed the animosity, and strongly suggested a 'come-to-Jesus' meeting.
Carlisle (PA) *Sentinel*, February 2005.

the smell test (US): a test used to determine the legitimacy or authenticity of something. If something passes the smell test, it passes muster.

to have something on lockdown (US): to have something completely under control or sewn up (originally a prison term).

can't scrap a lick (US): unable to put up a fight. There are many variants of the same formula (e.g. 'can't shoot/sing/act a lick'), all describing an ineptitude at something.

manbag

manbag: a man's handbag or purse, sometimes alternatively referred to as a **murse**.

clicktrance

clicktrance: the state induced by viewing large amounts of content on a website, involving multiple clicking of a computer mouse.

unschooling

unschooling: the teaching of a child at home rather than at school. Such a child is known as an **unschooler**.

furkid

furkid: a pet which serves as a child substitute. The term is a successor to 'animal guardian' and 'furbaby', both of which emerged in the 1990s. 'Furkid' is used by some animal lovers who feel that the word 'pet' suggests the idea of owning something, rather than describing the loving relationship that they have with their dog, cat, etc.

popstrology

popstrology: the theory that the song that was top of the music charts on the day a person was born influences their character.

Under duress, popstrology can even offer insights into the Bush Administration. Dick Cheney is an Artie Shaw ('Man of few words, curmudgeonly intellectual . . .'). Condoleezza Rice is an Eddie Fisher ('Lothario . . . . her staunch loyalty has to be deriving from some kind of opposition to that popstrological course').

The New Yorker, March 2005.

bluesnarfing

bluesnarfing: the use of wireless Bluetooth technology (which provides connections for all kinds of communication devices, such as between mobile phones and computers) to access a person's private data. In 2005, the mobile phone of model and actress Paris Hilton was attacked by 'snarfers' (in this case conceptual art outlaws) who posted Hilton's contact numbers and other private details on the Internet.

Just a few weeks ago, a security group calling themselves Flexilis made the news. One of their members stood next to the red carpet at the Academy Awards with a laptop and an antenna hidden in his backpack, and the results weren't exactly unsurprising: between 50 and 100 of the celebs were vulnerable to bluesnarfing.

securityfocus.com, March 2005.

hotsaucing

hotsaucing (also known as **tongue-spanking**)**:** the dabbing of a naughty child's tongue with hot and spicy Tabasco sauce. The technique is recommended to parents and teachers in the bestselling US manual 'Creative Correction: Extraordinary Ideas for Everyday Discipline'. Unsurprisingly, the term has attracted much controversy. In Virginia, 'hotsaucing' is legally actionable, but the practice is prevalent in rural America and among conservative Christians.

Hotsaucing, saucers will argue, is no worse than putting bitter aloe on fingernails to stop children biting them. Opponents will retort that hotsaucing, like all ritualised punishment, infringes George Bernard Shaw's golden rule: 'If you strike a child, take care that you strike it in anger.'

John Sutherland in *The Guardian*, September 2004.

farbulous

farbulous (a blend of 'far out' and 'fabulous')**:** a term of approval used to describe cutting-edge fashion—and those who wear it. The adjective is also used more specifically of or by re-enactors of historical episodes such as the Civil War, where it refers to clothing or accessories which post-date the historical period being role-played.

boomburbs

boomburbs (US)**:** a new kind of suburban-style settlement which is seeing significant growth in population and prosperity. Recent US census data suggests that some boomburbs are eclipsing big cities in their growth rate.

happy slapping

happy slapping: the recording, by groups of young people on their mobile phone cameras, of the slapping of a stranger in order to record their reaction. The subsequent pictures—which, according to *The Guardian*, have titles such as *Bitch Slap*, *Knockout Punch*, or *Bank Job*, depending on their content—are then forwarded to the phones of their friends using 3G wireless technology.

'Happy slapping' has apparently spread from the UK garage music scene to school playgrounds (as most fads do) and is now taking the nation by storm.

Engadget.com, April 2005.

About the size of it . . .

Size acceptance is an area in which language, as well as size, is being recalibrated. **BBWs**, or 'big beautiful women', and **FAs**, 'fat admirers', have hundreds of (**flabulous**) dedicated websites, offering **plus-size fashion** and designed for **supersize**, **husky**, or **zaftig** (a Yiddish word meaning 'plump' or 'juicy') women and those attracted to them, variously described as **BHMs** ('big hunky men') and **chubby-chasers**. The lexicon of such sites includes the agent noun **feeder** and the unusual construction **feedee**, controversial terms which describe the giving, and consensual taking, of large amounts of food for sexual gratification.

omnigooglization

omnigooglization: a term coined by the French press to describe American cultural domination, following the news that Google, the US search engine, is to offer online access to books currently housed in five of the English-speaking world's most prestigious libraries. The announcement reignited the fear on the part of the French that the influence of their language and culture is diminishing.

Minister Donnedieu also threw in his two ducats' worth about omnigooglization, saying that Google's method of ranking search results by user popularity is disgraceful, and reflective of an 'American system' of commercial capitalism.

Daily Pennsylvanian, April 2005.

frosting

frosting: stealing an unattended car which has been left with the engine running in order to warm it up.

Regulating Confusion: The Task of the Dictionary-Makers

3

I found our speech copious without order, and energetick without rules: wherever I turned my view, there was perplexity to be disentangled, and confusion to be regulated.

Samuel Johnson in his Preface to *A Dictionary of the English Language*.

2005 was the 250th anniversary of one of the greatest achievements in the recording of the English language. On 15 April 1755, Samuel Johnson's two-volume, 2,300 page *A Dictionary of the English Language* was published, only nine years after he began writing it in his cramped offices south of London's Fleet Street. Nine years in lexicographical terms is a remarkably short time, particularly for a work which had such lasting importance. It remained in print in its entirety for over a century, and new selections from the work continue to be published today.

Until the *Oxford English Dictionary* was completed in 1928, Johnson's work was the pre-eminent record of the English language. Although not the first, his dictionary was a landmark not only because Johnson was able successfully to put into practice the methods with which others were experimenting at the time, but also because he brought to the work such a distinctive and commanding literary voice.

While the first modern dictionaries began to appear in Europe during the Renaissance in the fifteenth and sixteenth centuries, England lagged behind its European neighbours and the first monolingual work (as opposed to bilingual Latin and English dictionaries) was not published until 1604. Robert Cawdrey's *A Table Alphabeticall* contained only 2,500 entries and was essentially a thesaurus or glossary of 'hard words'. Indeed 'dictionaries' in this early period tended to be predominantly lists of eccentric and specialized vocabulary. The need for greater comprehensiveness was observed by, amongst others, the philosopher David Hume, who wrote in 1741 that 'We have no Dictionary of our Language, and scarce a tolerable Grammar'.

◻

Over the course of the eighteenth century, dictionaries became more expansive. Johnson's most important predecessor, Nathan Bailey, was proof that lexicographers were starting to look beyond the narrow parameters of previous records of English to 'real' words—although of course it should be remembered that 'real' words in the eighteenth century did not include slang, dialect, and other 'low' words. Bailey's *Universal Etymological English Dictionary* was published in 1721 and was followed by the larger *Dictionarium Britannicum* in 1730, which was used as a starting point for Johnson's own dictionary. Johnson extended such beginnings quite dramatically.

◻

Before embarking on his project, Johnson set out his aims and convictions in his *Plan for a Dictionary*. He shared a belief held by many at the time that English was degenerating rapidly, and that a prescriptive (that is, one that 'prescribed' or dictated what language should be like rather than one which merely described it) record of correct language was needed to arrest the decline. He began his work at a time when language was changing rapidly, keeping pace with the dramatic social changes which were to lead to the Industrial Revolution and the expansion of the British Empire. Johnson's plan was part of a wider impulse to capture (and in doing so, regulate) the language in daily use, and on a scale not attempted before.

◻

It is instructive to compare the theoretical statements of Johnson's *Plan* with the views articulated in his *Preface* to the dictionary, written some eight years later. The experience of writing the Dictionary had taught him a great deal about language and about the impossibility of trying to 'fix' it and hold it in its 'proper' place. In the *Preface* his expressed aim was now to record language as it was rather than as he wanted it to be. He sought a regulation of language by consensus rather than by one single academy (as had been established in France), and he looked for such consensus in the most important writers of his time, from whom he selected his illustrations of usage. While the use of quotations in a dictionary was not entirely new, Johnson's prolific use of literary sources makes his work as much an anthology of English literature as a dictionary of definitions.

The 1980s British comedy series *Blackadder* included a spoof of Samuel Johnson presenting his dictionary to the royal court. Blackadder's invented words are, in their fancifulness, not too dissimilar from the eccentricities of dictionaries before Johnson's time.

JOHNSON: This book, sir, contains every word in our beloved language!

BLACKADDER: Every word, sir?

JOHNSON: Every word, sir!

BLACKADDER: Oh. Well, in that case, sir, I hope you will not object if I also offer the Doctor my most enthusiastic... contrafibularities.

JOHNSON: What?!

BLACKADDER: Contrafibularities, sir? It is a common word, down our way.

JOHNSON: Damn!

BLACKADDER: Oh, I'm sorry, sir. I'm anaspeptic, frasmotic, even compunctuous to have caused you such pericombobulation.

Johnson's Dictionary is a highly individual and, at times, eccentric work; the personality of its maker is evident throughout. Most modern dictionaries gain their colour in different ways: while their entries generally strive to be neutral in tone and descriptive in nature, their definitions are illustrated and informed by evidence from an extraordinarily broad spectrum of sources, ranging from scholarly journals to tabloid newspapers and chat rooms. *A Dictionary of the English Language* is very clearly the work of one man.

Yet in spite of the differences, much of the methodology used in today's lexicography—the use of illustrative quotations, the categorization of definitions into numbered senses—was already evident in Johnson's time. Debates over language and its state of health have also continued, and the calls for a regulator of language are still audible. It is to the chagrin of many that modern dictionaries reflect language and its changes of direction rather than prescribe its correct usage.

The following entries, taken from Johnson's *A Dictionary of the English Language* and the *Oxford Dictionary of English* (2005) respectively, reflect the development of lexicography in the period between Johnson's time and our own. They include some good illustrations of the definition style of the 1755 work, of the information reflecting the beliefs of the time (that, for example, a tarantula's bite is cured only by music), and the tone in which that information was conveyed.

1755

harridan, noun [corrupted from *haridelle*. a worn-out worthless horse] A decayed strumpet.

2005

harridan, noun
a strict, bossy, or belligerent old woman: *a bullying old harridan*. [Origin: late 17th century (originally slang): perhaps from French *haridelle* 'old horse'.]

1755

to hiccough, verb
To sob with convulsion of the stomach.

2005

hiccup (also hiccough), noun
an involuntary spasm of the diaphragm and respiratory organs, with a

sudden closure of the glottis and a characteristic gulping sound: *then she got hiccups*.

———————

1755

oats, noun
A grain, which in England is generally given to horses, but in Scotland supports the people.

2005

oats, noun
the grain yielded by the oat plant, used as food.

———————

1755

billingsgate, noun
[A cant word, borrowed from *Bilingsgate* in London, a place where there is always a crowd of low people, and frequent brawls and foul language.] Ribaldry, foul language.

There stript, fair rhet'rick languish'd on the ground
And shameful bilingsgate her robes adorn
Dunciad.

2005

Billingsgate
A London fish market dating from the 16th century. In 1982 the market moved to the Isle of Dogs in the East End.

———————

1755

tarantula, noun
An insect whose bite is cured only by musick.

2005

tarantula, noun

a very large hairy spider found chiefly in tropical and subtropical America, some kinds of which are able to catch small lizards, frogs, and birds.

Not surprisingly, the 1755 work also includes words which have fallen largely out of use. Their colour and—in some cases at least—usefulness make their demise (personally) regrettable. A few of them are collected here.

backfriend, noun
A friend backwards; that is, an enemy in secret.

to clapperclaw, verb
To tonguebeat; to scold.

bellygod, noun
A glutton; one who makes a god of his belly.

jack pudding, noun
A zani; a merry Andrew*.
(*described in Johnson's dictionary as 'a buffoon')

mundungous, adjective
Stinking tobacco.

to nubble, verb
To bruise with handycuffs.

garlickeater, noun
A mean fellow.

mullgrubs, noun
Twisting of the guts.

pickthank, noun
An officious fellow, who does what he is not desired. A whispering parasite.

flapdragon, noun
A play in which they catch raisins out of burning brandy and, extinguishing them by closing the mouth, eat them.

to wamble, verb
To roll with nausea and sickness. It is used of the stomach.

to scranch, verb
To grind somewhat crackling between the teeth. The Scots retain it.

to prog, verb
1. To rob; to steal.
2. To shift meanly for provisions. A low word.

pundle, noun
A short and fat woman.

Lastly, while words may have survived into the present day, some of them have taken on very different meanings from those of 1755. (There are exceptions, such as **pash**, a kiss, which recently re-entered English from Australia together with offshoots such as **pash rash**—sore lips resulting from too much kissing—while **cit**, an unruly citizen, sounds decidedly modern). Comparisons with modern definitions offer interesting glimpses of how language evolves. The following are extracts from entries in Johnson's dictionary and the current edition of the *Oxford Dictionary of English*.

1755
high-flier, noun
One that carries his opinion to extravagance.

2005
high-flyer (also high-flier), noun
a person who is or has the potential to be extremely successful, especially academically or in business.

––––––––––

1755
aphrodisiacal, aphrodisiac, adjective
Relating to the venereal disease.

2005

aphrodisiac, noun

a food, drink, or other thing that stimulates sexual desire: *power is the ultimate aphrodisiac.*

aphrodisiacal, adjective

of the nature of an aphrodisiac, stimulating sexual desire.

1755

autopsy, noun

Ocular demonstration; seeing a thing one's self.
In those that have forked tails, autopsy convinceth us, that it hath this use.
Ray on the Creation.

2005

autopsy, noun

a post-mortem examination to discover the cause of death or the extent of disease.
[Origin: mid 17th century (in the sense 'personal observation'): from French *autopsie* or modern Latin *autopsia*, from Greek, from *autoptēs* 'eyewitness', from *autos* 'self' + *optos* 'seen'.]

1755

funk, noun

A stink. A low word.

2005

funk, noun

• a style of popular dance music of US black origin, based on elements of blues and soul and having a strong rhythm that typically accentuates the first beat in the bar.
• North American, informal, dated: a strong musty smell of sweat or tobacco.
[Origin: early 17th century (in the sense 'musty smell'): perhaps from French dialect *funkier* 'blow smoke on', based on Latin *fumus* 'smoke'.]

1755

pedant, noun
A schoolmaster.

2005

pedant, noun
a person who is excessively concerned with minor details and rules or with displaying academic learning. [Origin: late 16th century, perhaps from the first element of Latin *paedegogus*, denoting a slave who accompanied a child to school.]

When Johnson began his monumental work, he was motivated by the need to order 'the boundless chaos of a living speech'. Eight years on he wrote of his realization of the futility of any such attempt: 'Sounds are too volatile and subtle for legal restraints; to enchain syllables, and to lash the wind, are equally the undertakings of pride.' The dilemma of letting a language evolve as its users wish it to, while at the same time maintaining order and clarity, is one which continues to preoccupy us today. If it is a debate which is unlikely to see any real resolution, we must be grateful to Johnson for a unique record of one stage in our language's history, and for one which is so eminently readable even today.

Ever-Increasing Circles: The Making of New Words

4

Chavistocrat: what to call the super-posh when they dress and act as if they would be happier hanging around outside McDonald's.

Tatler magazine, March 2005.

Mr Dyson has one more hill to climb. To say 'Let me Dyson the carpet' does not have the same onomatopoeic resonance as to Hoover it.

Leader in *The Guardian*, 23 February 2005 (in fact the verb 'to dyson' looks to be gaining currency).

This book is full of characters who didn't just live in the fast lane but populated their very own ring road, completely bypassing straightsville.

Review on the BBC website of Jimmy McDonough's biography of Neil Young, 2005.

Discover Your Inner Skinny.

Harpers and Queen magazine, March 2005.

Every year, the editors of the *Oxford English Dictionary* receive countless letters requesting that a particular new word be included in its vast records of the English language. These words have for the most part been created and used by the letter-writer and by their immediate community. For the majority of them, their quest will end in disappointment. It is not enough for a word to be colourful, clever, useful, or simply new: for any new item to merit inclusion in a dictionary, it has to be *used*, and widely.

The criteria applied by lexicographers to new words are strict. Traditionally, for the *OED*, evidence is required of a word having acquired widespread currency over a number of years, either generally or within a specific area. There are exceptions: **chav**, which exploded onto the scene in 2004, has gained a place in Oxford dictionaries much sooner, but there is little doubt that the word meets the fundamental requirement of broad usage.

The origins of the words we use every day have in some cases been lost over their lifetime. Others have simply never been explained definitively and can only be conjectured at. It may seem surprising that the origin of a new word should be uncertain, since the passage of time cannot be blamed for its obscurity. But in fact it is often extremely difficult to trace a word back to its very first use, especially if it is an informal word—in the end we can only offer theories.

Equally disappointing to some is the statistic that only one per cent of all new words are, in fact, entirely 'new'. The vast majority of neologisms are new takes on the old. The effect, however, is far from one of repetitiveness. The ability to renew itself is one of the fascinations of language; hundreds of words or phrases which appeared to be beyond recall turn out to have been merely dormant.

Retakes and revivals

The giving of new meanings to old words is one of the most frequent triggers of language change. It is particularly dramatic in teenage slang, where words of disapproval are subverted to mean the opposite (for example *bad*, *random*, and *heavy*). To call the results 'new' is perhaps misleading, but the process underscores the circularity of language, and the fact that 'totally' new words are rarer than we might think.

Words can also be resurrected from the past with their meanings intact: the true age of some of the fashionable words of the moment can often surprise: *hip*, for example, dates back to 1904, while *groovy* pre-dates the swinging sixties by some thirty years.

Language on the move

The ever-increasing lexicon relating to 'chav' (**chavette**; **chavtastic**; **chavvish**; **chavdom**) is testimony to another mechanism behind new word coining, whereby one word forms the base for new words by the addition of suffixes such as '-dom', '-ness', and '-ish'. The extent to which a word has such adaptability can be one of the indicators of its future survival. The term **blog** (a contraction of 'weblog', describing an online personal diary or journal), for example, has spawned a host of related terms describing activities in the **blogosphere/blogdom**, including **blogroll** (a part of a blog listing links to other blogs), **phlog** (a photo blog), **vlog** (a video blog), and **moblog** (a blog which can be updated via mobile phone).

There are occasionally unlikely survivors: the 2003 acronym **MVVD** (for 'male vertical volume drinker') seemed then too clumsy to stand the test of time. Nonetheless, in government circles today the even longer **HVVDE** (for a 'high vertical volume drinking establishment') is now a common shorthand for large pubs with more standing than sitting room.

New words are often the result of linguistic playfulness, often in an effort to entertain: journalists in 2005 spoke of the current tendency to **puddingerize** (to get fat), and of the ubiquitous process of **Starbuckization**. Such creative manipulation is also to be found in the fictional worlds of television and novels; the results may often enter the vocabulary of the real world and eventually lose their original associations, some thereby changing their meaning. The word **correctamundo** has outlived the TV show *Happy Days* which spawned it, just as the history of the phrase **luvvly jubbly**, based on a 1950s advertising slogan for the frozen triangular-shaped orange drink 'jubbly', has been lost, while the term thrives as a general expression of approval thanks to the TV comedy *Only Fools and Horses* and to its more recent take-up by TV chef Jamie Oliver.

Mixing and matching: the 'blend'

The mechanisms behind the making of new words are very often the result of taking parts of existing words and putting them together in different ways. 'Blending' is one example of this, and the results are often flippant and tongue-in-cheek. Currently, pets appear to be popular territory for blending, both genetically and linguistically; in particular, the word 'poodle' seems to offer infinite comic possibilities.

cockapoodle (also **cockapoo**) (= cocker spaniel + poodle)

labradoodle (= Labrador + poodle)

goldendoodle (= golden retriever + poodle)

peekaboo (= Pekinese + poodle)

schnoodle (= poodle + schnauzer)

maltepoo (= Maltese terrier + poodle)

Expanding wordage

In the surreal fictional world of the TV series *Buffy the Vampire Slayer*, a key component of 'Buffyspeak' was the prolific use of the suffix **-age**. Buffy and her friends would speak of **blood-coughage**, **slayage**, and **red tape-age**, and in doing so set in motion a trend which is still continuing after the series has ended. Football commentators speak of **maimage**, musicians of **riffage** (guitar riffing), while **bronzage** (tanning), **diskage** (disk space on a computer), **stinkage** (a bad smell), **tweakage** (tweaking), and **webbage** (web-based content or terminology), are all well documented.

Variations on a theme

When news broke in 2004 of British football hero Wayne Rooney's liaison with a prostitute, one headline became inevitable: **Rooneygate**! The player became one in a long line of names which have earned (willingly or otherwise) a pairing with **-gate** since the original Watergate scandal, and the formula shows no signs of waning (see *The Language of Events*, pages 5–10). Meanwhile in 2005, Prince Charles' alleged annoyance over the organizational difficulties besetting his wedding to Camilla Parker Bowles was too much temptation for *The Mirror* which ran the simple headline 'Heir Rage', proving that **-rage** combinations also retain their popularity.

Other highly productive combining forms of the moment include:

-licious: bootylicious, babelicious, chocolicious, mochalicious

-babble: psychobabble, technobabble, blondebabble, diplobabble, Barbiebabble, ecobabble, Blairbabble

-head: petrolhead, musclehead, pointyhead, beathead

-ville: mootville, yawnsville, sleazeville, smashedville

-fest: gloomfest, shagfest, vibefest, footiefest, clickfest, hackfest, bitchfest

-tastic: poptastic, funktastic, retrotastic, tinseltastic, tobaccoatastic, dudetastic, blubtastic

über- (super, the height of something, from the German): **überdoll, überpedant, überchav, überblogger, überhipster**

Skipping classes

The swapping over of a word from one part-of-speech category to another is currently a common generator of new words. Teenagers talk of things which 'give me **a happy**' (thanks again to Buffy), while the fictional 'gangsta' rapper Ali G speaks of 'looking like **a homeless**'. Other recent examples of adjectives becoming nouns in this way include **famouses** for famous people, **tragics** for 'anoraks' or 'nerds', and **the starvings** for those affected by famine (a misrepresentation of the collective 'the starving'). It is perhaps worth noting that not all such creations are new: the use of the noun 'a religious' to denote someone devoted to religious life dates back as far as 1225.

Nouns in turn can become verbs: one member of the British All-Party Republican Group spoke early in 2005 of the British public having been

'**PR-ed** into accepting Camilla', while the process of **supersizing** is now as established linguistically as it appears to be in the West's consumer culture. Other nouns which are actively engaging as verbs are **to cowboy**, **to nanny**, **to steamroller**, and even **to bro**, the latter being a term used by Nike to define its marketing strategy of appealing to black youth. One of the defining terms of the early 'noughties', **bling**, has crossed over into almost every part-of-speech category, from the initial noun (also called **bling-bling**) to a verb ('he really blings it up'), an adjective ('I've got to get those shoes; they're so bling-blingy'), and an adverb ('she's dressed up well bling').

The term **ASBO** (for an antisocial behaviour order) was a hot talking point in 2004. The abbreviation quickly rooted itself in the language as an acronym. At least one journalist turned it into an adjective: 'When those at the top turn ASBO, who's going to tell the axe-wielding ASBOs to drop the axe?' (J. J. King, *channel4.com*).

I ♥, you ♥, she ♥

One of the more unusual shifts in recent times involves the word 'heart'. In most newspapers and online accounts the heart symbol in the 2005 film title I ♥ *Huckabees* was transcribed as 'heart'. While not the first instance of the use of the heart symbol (graffiti and bumper stickers bearing the legend I ♥ NY/CA/my cat etc. have been around since the 1970s or earlier), the film sparked off a whole succession of uses of 'heart' as a verb, meaning simply 'to love' ('I heart my boo'). The move from symbol to word has not diluted the sentimentality of the heart: as John Sutherland wrote in *The Guardian*, 'There is...something tacky about ♥—rather like the Mr Smiley face. It has too much of what REM sarcastically call a "shiny happy people" feel to it.'

Language on the make

Occasionally the name of a highly successful brand of product becomes synonymous with the product itself. There are numerous examples of this from the past: *lino*, *nylon*, *hoover*, *Tupperware*, *Pyrex*, *biro*, and *Kleenex* all have (or once had) trademark status, but their names have also acquired a general status and are used even where referring to other brands of the same product. While the *Guardian* leader quoted at the beginning of this section may be right in saying that James Dyson's success with vacuum cleaners will not necessarily guarantee linguistic permanence, the verb **to dyson** is in fact already in evidence.

A more recent example of trademarked terms slipping into the mainstream is the word **Orgasmatron**. The word may have been coined in the Woody Allen film *Sleeper*, but has recently re-emerged after being trademarked as the name of a sex-aid device aimed at remedying female sexual dysfunction. 'Orgasmatron' has very quickly become a figure of speech for anything potent and highly charged. The blogs of players of computer games and MUDs (multi-action dungeon games) are full of references to 'orgasmatronic' graphics and characters.

Absorbing English

It has been estimated that about half of all English words have, over the history of the language, been 'borrowed' from non-Anglo-Saxon languages. These words, known as 'loanwords', are responsible for some of the most colourful and exotic vocabulary items in use in English today. One area in which English is most rapidly assimilating from abroad is food and drink. Recent absorptions include:

limoncello: an Italian lemon liqueur.

maltagliati (from Italian meaning 'badly cut'): a type of irregularly shaped pasta.

raciones (Spanish): larger helpings of tapas.

sofrito (Spanish meaning 'lightly fried or sautéed'): a combination of onion, green pepper, garlic, tomato, coriander, thyme, and oil used as a staple in many Puerto Rican dishes.

gandules (Caribbean): pigeon peas (often served with rice).

crema (Italian): the creamy head on espresso coffee.

digestivo (Italian): an aperitif.

Out of nowhere

If very few of the new words entering English are completely new inventions, those that do make it often have a slightly magical quality as a result. Aside from brand names, and the scientific or technical terminology required to fill linguistic gaps, there are a small number of words which seem to have been created out of thin air.

Muggle is one of many intriguing words which inhabit the works of J. K. Rowling, the creator of Harry Potter, and a term which enchants both by virtue of its associations with Harry's magical world and by its own onomatopoeic resonance. Used to mean a 'non-wizard', or someone without magical powers, it has taken hold in the world of fantasy games and is used by gamers to denote someone who is computer illiterate or lacking in skill (a *luser* in fact—a blend of 'loser' and 'user'). The *OED* lists previous senses of 'muggle': over time it has variously meant 'a tail resembling that of a fish' (circa 1275), a young woman or sweetheart (1608), and later, in the 1920s, a marijuana joint.

Another recent example of a word with no easily traceable origin is **doobie**, a cannabis cigarette. The term is first recorded in the *OED* in 1967 as part of Black American slang, and it is best known as part of the name of the US 1970s rock band the *Doobie Brothers*. Its ultimate origin, however, is unknown.

Choice cuts

Abbreviations, acronyms, and initialisms make up a further category of neologizing, and it is one which appears to be on the increase. Texting and emails have produced highly truncated languages of their own in which abbreviations are the norm, while mobile phone technology appears to be creating new initialisms almost daily. Sometimes a string of initialisms on the same theme emerges: **DWI**, for example, meaning 'driving while impaired', now sits alongside **DWY**: driving while yelling (into a mobile phone), and **DWB**: driving while black. The last illustrates the use of the formula to describe the alleged police practice of stopping drivers out of racial motives. In one episode of the political drama *The West Wing*, a supreme court nominee of Hispanic origin is pulled over by the police and jailed, prompting the following dialogue:

C.J.: Then what was he pulled over for?

SAM: Driving while Hispanic.

It is almost impossible to quantify the rate at which new words appear. Many believe that we are experiencing a time of unprecedented neological enthusiasm, and that new words are being created at a faster rate than ever, but this is a claim that has been made for earlier periods such as the Elizabethan age. Perhaps the point is that we are far more aware of new words, thanks to the new media available to us—media which also allow a new word to gain exposure in a fraction of the time it would have taken even a few decades ago.

Words Apart: 1905 vs 2005 **5**

Like the growth rings of a tree, our vocabulary bears witness to our past.

John Algeo, *Fifty Years Among the New Words*, 1991.

A study of words separated by a hundred years provides an instant snapshot of the myriad of processes involved in language evolution. Among the hundreds of words coined in the years 1905 and 2005 are examples both of giant leaps of imagination and of remarkable consistency in the intervening century. Within the picture is evidence too of the circularity of English: of the way in which vocabulary can fade, only to re-emerge strongly when needed. When we compare the neologisms of the two years directly, we may be astonished by the long history of words which seem highly topical today, and intrigued by others which have stayed uniquely linked to their time.

The first decade of the twentieth century saw the beginnings of changes which would revolutionize many aspects of life. The motor car was establishing its importance and demanding a new vocabulary to describe it. The **foot-clutch**, **road atlas**, **petrol pump**, **traffic lane**, **motor veil** (the latest female fashion accessory, necessary to protect the face in the early open vehicles), and even the **motorphobe**, all entered the lexicon of 1905, a hundred years before we acquired **Chelsea tractor** (see below). Meanwhile, the scientific and technical advances of the late nineteenth century were continuing at great speed and were about to transform the areas of energy, medicine, and warfare. **Hydroelectricity**, **hormones**, **mine-sweeping**, and **bomb-making** made their appearance in the same year. The term **genetics**, while not new—in the late nineteenth century it had been used as a definition for 'the study of natural development when not complicated by human interference'—shifted to reflect the new scientific study of heredity and variation. At the age of 26, Albert Einstein published three papers explaining **Brownian motion**, the **photoelectric effect**, and his **special theory of relativity**.

On 13 October 1905, Christabel Pankhurst and Annie Kenney heckled at a Liberal Party meeting: 'Will the Liberal government, if returned, give votes to women?' Christabel was subsequently jailed for obstruction, and the militant campaign by 'suffragists' was initiated. The term **suffragist**, coined in the mid 1880s, was replaced in 1906 by **suffragette**. (The arc of the feminine suffix '-ette' is an interesting example of language change. Embraced in 1906 for its reflection of the empowering of women, it came in the twentieth century to be seen as diminutive and patronizing. Today it is re-emerging as anything but a reductive term, as in **ladette** and **dudette**.)

1905 also saw the advent of **big business** and **high finance**, while the **property market** boasted the opportunities of the new **garden suburb**. The latest **news stories** and **fashion journals** were read in one of the burgeoning **coffee bars** (serving **café con leche**), and the therapeutic effects of **mind healers**, **beauty doctors**, and **gospel songs** were all recognized in the language. In sport, the New Zealand rugby team was given the nickname **All Blacks** by British journalists at the beginning of the team's 1905 tour of Britain; the term soon became semi-official.

On 1 December 1905, Arthur Balfour resigned as Prime Minister. He remains the last premier to cede power to the leader of the opposition without having been defeated in a general election. Appropriately, the term **wind of change** was coined in the same year, used by Sarojini Naidu in her poem *To a Buddha Sitting On A Lotus* ('The wind of change for ever blows/Across the tumult of our way'). The phrase was later to become fixed in the language, after the British Prime Minister Harold Macmillan used it in a speech to the South African Parliament in 1960, when he spoke of 'the wind of change blowing through our continent' [Africa].

At the beginning of the twentieth century, words from other languages were, as always, making their mark on the language. 1905 saw the adoption into English of the verb **frou-frou** from the French, meaning 'to move about with the rustling of draperies', and of German words such as

hochgeboren and **Lebensraum**. The latter term, meaning 'living space', denoted territory which the Germans believed was needed for natural development. It was later to take on sinister connotations when it became an integral part of the Nazi manifesto.

Zeitgeist or zeitfrei?

Some words, while not obsolete, remain stamped with the mark of their times. Others have moved on in step with their environment to the extent that their history goes unquestioned.

Frozen in time:

old sport

humdinger

top-hole

skidoo and **skedaddle**

whizzo

umpty (an indefinite number, usually a large one)

A hundred years strong:

think tank

yeah

Braxton Hicks

top drawer

a jolly

happy as Larry

Sunday supplements

troubleshooter

operative (a detective or secret-service agent)

loan shark

floating voter

In addition to those words which remain as strongly topical today as a hundred years ago, are those which speak eloquently of the preoccupations of their time.

1905

come-on: a swindler. The term began in the US as a slang term for a con man. The first citation in the *Oxford English Dictionary* for a sexual come-on is from the 1940s, although the term meant a general enticement or invitation to approach as early as 1902.

The general appearance of the man caused the officer to become suspicious, and he soon learned that Dates was a come-on.

New York Evening Post, 1905.

trunk murder: a murder after which the body is hidden in a luggage trunk and often then sent to a distant destination. This method of disposing of a body was apparently common at this time.

Trunk murder. How the bodies were found.

Daily Mail headline, 1905.

stagger juice: strong drink.

Lor! Boss! If we didn't drink the stagger juice no one would.

Alexander Macdonald, *In the Land of Pearl and Gold*, 1907.

Mickey Doo (also known as a **Mick Dooley**): a derogatory reference to someone. The term, which originated as New Zealand slang and which plays on a typically Irish name, survives today, particularly in personal weblogs. A **Mickey Doolan**, meanwhile, is New Zealand slang for a Catholic.

roughy: a rough or rowdy person; a brawler; a hooligan. The term originated in Scottish and Irish dialect.

news butch: a seller of newspapers, sweets, etc. on a train. The term, from US slang, is short for a 'news butcher': 'butcher' being a common word at the time for a vendor.

pomato: a name used by Luther Burbank (1849–1926), American horticulturist, for the fruit of a hybrid potato, which resembled a tomato. The fruit and the name both fizzled out and were not revived until the

1970s when the term was used again to designate the result of attempts to hybridize the potato and the tomato. It was one of the first portmanteau 'blends' coined to describe the creation of hybrid species.

pogrom: an organized massacre intended to destroy a person or entire order. The term originally applied to massacres, organized in Russia, directed against the Jews in the 1880s. It is a borrowing from Russian and means 'devastation or destruction'. A new wave of pogroms in 1903 propelled the word into English.

smog: fog intensified by smoke. In Britain the term came to be particularly associated with the severe and deadly smog which covered London in the early 1950s. The *OED* cites a 1905 article from the *Globe* newspaper which reported that:

The other day, at a meeting of the Public Health Congress, Dr. Des Voeux did a public service in coining a new word for the London fog, which was referred to as 'smog', a compound of 'smoke' and 'fog'.

slummocker: an awkward or careless person. The term was an offshoot of the older word 'slammakin', meaning a slovenly or clumsy person. It was coined by George Bernard Shaw in a letter to the critic James Gibbons Huneker, following a critical review of *Man and Superman*:

You will never be anything but a clever slummocker in America.

big-sticker: someone or something who performs a 'big-stick', a display of force or power. The term is probably an allusion to a speech made by Theodore Roosevelt in 1900, in which he said: 'I have always been fond of the West African proverb: "Speak softly and carry a big stick; you will go far."' In 1912 Rudyard Kipling wrote that 'the secret of power is not the big stick...it's the liftable stick'.

There is nothing in the British record to compare with Roosevelt's robust big-stickism in the Alaska boundary case.

The Spectator, 1926.

2005

hooptie (Black American slang)**:** a large, old model of car, sometimes also called a 'hoopty-whoopty'. The term sits alongside others used in black slang and in particular in rap lyrics, including **trap cars** (customized cars associated with drug dealers or pimps, often with tinted windows, lowered suspension, and expensive sound systems), **whips** (fast, expensive cars such as Aston Martins), and **shorts** (small, compact cars).

bliki (also **bloki**): a blog that can be edited like a wiki (a website which allows users to add and edit content). After an article is posted to the blog it can be added to by a group of users authorized to do so by the bliki's originator or, in some cases, by anyone at all.

cuddle party: a fee-paying party at which invitees stroke and cuddle each other, in a non-sexual way, to induce feelings of well-being. The group, supervised by 'cuddle caddies', form a 'puppy pile'. Each participant must ask permission before touching another, and each has the right to refuse. The phenomenon, founded by 'sex and romance coach' Reid Mihalko, began in the US but has since spread to Canada and looks set to arrive in the UK.

No sex please, this is a cuddle party.
Headline to an article in the *Sunday Times*, July 2004.

mobisode: a short, exclusive episode of a soap or drama which is viewable on the new generation of mobile phones.

podcast: a digital recording of a radio broadcast or similar programme, made available on the Internet for downloading to a personal audio player.

oppie (acronym for 'organic professionals'): a professional who downshifts to the countryside while retaining urban accessories.

In the Fashion & Style section of Sunday's New York Times, Alex Williams finally combined 'organic' and 'professional' to make 'oppie', the downshifting, higher-consciousness-reaching cousin of the yuppie.
the green life blog, 2005.

protirement (a blend of 'proactive' and 'retirement'): the act of leaving the workplace in order to find something more fulfilling. The term was coined in the US by Frederic M. Hudson, the founder of a work/life balance institute. Those who take protirement are 'protirers' or are 'protired'.

Without a private income, the protirer should be warned that there is a good chance that he will end up back in the office with his tail between his legs—and at a lower rung on the management ladder.
The Times, 2005.

Chelsea tractor: a derogatory term for a four-by-four vehicle used for short distances within a town or city. The cars, often used by moneyed professionals driving their children to school (in areas such as London's Chelsea), have been much criticized by environmentalists and others in the community for being damaging to the environment and generally antisocial in city streets. They are the British equivalent of the equally controversial American **SUVs** (sports utility vehicles).

Terminator guns for the Chelsea Tractor.

Headline for an article in *The Observer*, September 2004, describing Arnold Schwarzenegger's backing of tough new legislation in his state of California to reduce emissions by sports utility vehicles.

bromance (a blend of 'brother' and 'romance'): a non-sexual relationship between men, particularly in the first 'rush' of a new friendship. A meeting between such men is known as a **man date**.

We intertwined our arms before taking our first sip. People thought we were gay and we had to explain the principle of bromance to them.

Extract from a personal weblog, 2005.

twixter: people between the age of 20 and 30 who are still living at home and with no settled employment. The term refers to their being 'betwixt' childhood and adulthood. Similar terms of the last decade or so include the blends **kidult** and **adultescent**, and the plural acronym **kippers** (for 'kids in parents' pockets eroding retirement savings').

Parlez-Vous Twixter? This stage of life isn't solely an American phenomenon. It's popping up around the world under different names.

Time magazine, 2005.

A few fizzlers

The following are some of the coinages of 1905 which ultimately lacked the stamina to survive much beyond their time.

cerealist: someone who advocates a cereal diet.

to get a bun on (1901): to get drunk. Its origins, unfortunately, remain obscure.

auto-cycle: an alternative name for motorcycle. It survived into the middle of the twentieth century before fading from view.

Lizzie: a lesbian. The term was later used to describe an effeminate man.

wifing: the activity or condition of being a good housewife. Like 'slummocker' (above), the term was coined by George Bernard Shaw, here in reference to his own mother. The word has resurfaced in recent times but has changed to reflect new social attitudes and is today invariably used with heavy irony.

Bigging It Up and Playing It Down: Euphemism and Exaggeration

6

And when he brought us the glad tidings of the 'multi-agency Reflex Taskforce', they fell about in ersatz hysteria, since everyone knows that 'taskforce' is just a form of words that makes a committee sound more dynamic.
Simon Hoggart in *The Guardian*, February 2005, reporting on the Home Secretary Charles Clarke's presentation to the Commons of government strategies on immigration.

Precautionary principle is really just bureaucrat-speak for 'cover your ass'.
Ross Clark in the *Saturday Times*, February 2005.

There is a marked trend in current English usage towards inflated language: words and phrases which exaggerate in order to emphasize. From the habitual use of such fillers as **totally**, **well**, and **so**, to the jargon of the workplace with its talk of **empowerment**, the **visionary process**, and **passion statements**, the evidence of 'talking up' is everywhere. Linguistic extravagance of this kind may also operate as a form of euphemism, although here the aim is to 'big up' (to use a favourite term of the moment) rather than downplay.

In his study of *The Language Instinct*, the linguist Steven Pinker describes the 'euphemism treadmill', whereby euphemisms gradually assume the same force as the term they are camouflaging, and so need to be replaced. The same process can be seen more generally, when some words are used to the point of exhaustion and need replacing with others in order to maintain their strength of expression. This is particularly true of references to extreme emotion or belief. Whereas the term **incandescent**

with rage once carried the power of an impressive image, less clichéd alternatives such as **sulphuric anger** are now making their claim. The figurative sense of **putrid**, which dates back to the late nineteenth and early twentieth century, is also making a comeback as a general intensifying adjective, and may follow in the footsteps of the now weakened British usage 'rotten'. The writer Sara Jeannette Duncan showed some prescience in 1902 when she gave one character in her novel *Those Delightful Americans* the line: 'Last night at billiards you first said your luck was "rotten", and then you got excited and declared it was "putrid".'

The perception that many of our stock idioms and phrases are devalued does not always lead to replacement. Words which previously had sufficient power in themselves are attracting prefixes such as **über-**, **ova-**, or **mega-** ('übercreepy', 'ova-wicked', 'megafraud') in order to re-energize them.

In the US, the word **superhero** is threatening to supplant **hero**, such is the frequency with which the latter is used. In April 2005, a woman named Ashley Smith persuaded a convicted murderer to turn himself in to the police after he sought refuge at her house. She was widely described as a hero. Some commentators have started to fight a rearguard action over this devaluing tendency. In his column for the *New York Daily News*, Neil Steinberg commented that 'the word should be reserved for the truly worthy, both to keep language from losing all meaning and to honor genuine heroes'. If Ashley Smith is a hero, he continued, then to use the same description for the soldiers killed in Iraq, or the firefighters who gave their lives for others on 9/11, becomes meaningless.

Linguistic 'bigging up' falls into three broad groups: linguistic grandiosity, elaborate euphemism, and tautology. The first involves simple exaggeration. In politics, consultants given responsibility for certain areas are called **tsars** (Britain has, for example, both a **drug tsar** and an **ASBO tsar**). Meanwhile, new coinages using the suffix **-meister** are proliferating, as in **blogmeister**, **jargonmeister**, **scoremeister**. Cut-price stores selling cheap, high-turnover goods are known as **value retailers**. **Supercities** and **civic pioneers** are the new focus of the political strategists, while 'New' (as in **New Labour**, **New Emotionalism**, **New Localism**) adds an ideological gloss which the original term is felt to lack. In business, **action items**, **thoughtware**, and **bandwidth** refer respectively to things to do, things we know about, and time, while **uptitling**, the technique of giving workers elevated job titles, is thriving: cases have allegedly been found of receptionists receiving the official title of **head of verbal communications**, while supermarket shelf-stackers are known as **stock replenishment executives** and post-room helpers as **dispatch services facilitators**.

Even the language of weather is subject to strange forms of inflation. Forecasters speak of cloud systems **fringing** the Pennines, while **weather** itself has become synonymous with 'interesting' weather, such as downpours or snowstorms (or **the wet stuff** and **the white stuff**), as in **we're in for a lot of weather** this week. Pathetic fallacy may also feature, as when storms are said to **take aim**, or to be **packing a punch**.

The elaboration of menu writers, as of estate agents, leading to the use of flowery and affected jargon, is well known. Today's culinary experiences, many the result of **molecular gastronomy**, include flavoured **foams** (such as **l'air de parmesan**), **emulsions**, and **infusions**, while vegetables, meat, and fish come **crisped**, **seared**, **glazed**, **truffled**, and **lacquered**. Chefs **steam off** or **bake down** their creations. Chocolates are **enrobed** or **handcrafted**; their outer layers **hug** their fillings. Freshness is no longer a given: **seasonal**, **dew-fresh**, **market fresh**, and **local** are often boasted as an added bonus. In 2005 the film *Sideways* raised the profile of fine wines such as Pinot Noir and with them the creative lexicon of wine-tasting (the film included the memorable verdict of one wine as **quaffable, but not transcendent**). In wine-speak, the noun plus '-y' formula produces an infinite number of descriptors, including **seafoody**, **flabby**, **gamy**, **reedy**, **grippy**, and **buttery**.

In the second category of linguistic over-egging, the inflationary principle operates as euphemism. In one episode of the presidential drama *The West Wing*, the Chief of Staff's secretary, who refers to a meeting as being about 'ways to fight a possible recession', is asked not to use the word 'recession' in the White House. When she demands to know what language she should use instead, the response she receives is **the robust economy meeting**. Such sidestepping is noticeable in business jargon too, where **falling forward** means learning from your mistakes, and the **recalibration** of personnel is tantamount to firing them. Governments, meanwhile, no longer speak of 'public spending', rather of **public investment**, and an issue is **nuanced** rather than complicated.

There is one further area of supersized language: the adding to an utterance of a second word which means almost exactly the same thing as the first. This practice of tautology is particularly common in sports commentary: the footballer Wayne Rooney, for example, is regularly praised by commentators for his **grit and determination**, his **strength and power**, and for his **vision and awareness**. During the 2005 London Marathon the eventual winner Paula Radcliffe was described as showing tremendous **endurance and stamina**, while during the World Snooker Championship the most important quality for a player was cited as **focus and concentration**.

The current trend of upgrading words which are perceived to be worn out might suggest an alternative process of language evolution, whereby vocabulary is built up rather than replaced. Not for the first time: in the 1950s the word **heart-throb**, sparked by the public passion for film stars, was so overused that it lost its specificity and became a term meaning 'delightful': the *Daily Telegraph* in 1948 wrote of 'a heart-throb of a hat'. Today, it has shrunk back to the original noun. What will happen once these new 'überwords' are themselves exhausted is hard to predict; perhaps we will return to the originals, and make linguistic 'downshifting' the new order.

Dog-Whistling in the Wind: Political Talk

7

Blair rips open his shirt, which may or may not be from Paul Smith, and allows members of the public to flay him with knotty switches on national media outlets.

Zoe Williams in *The Guardian*, March 2005, on Tony Blair's so-called 'masochism strategy' (see overleaf).

You have as much chance of hearing an unusual turn of phrase from a politician as you would from a player interview on Football Focus. That is, about once every four-and-a-half seasons.

Tim Franks in his article *The Fall of Rhetoric* for the BBC, 2005.

Please do not call us Tories.

A plea said to have been made by the Conservative Party's head of broadcasting to TV stations, the worry being it might confuse voters. The word 'Tory' is a seventeenth-century word deriving from the Irish *toraidhe*, which means 'outlaw' or 'robber'. It has served the Conservative Party since Disraeli's time.

The phrase 'cool Britannia' became uncool for Tony, but once a dedicated follower of fashion, always so....Among segments of our electorate, blue-collar workers aren't cool. Among cars, Rovers aren't cool.

Matthew Parris in the Opinion column of *The Times*, April 2005, on the closing of the car manufacturer MG Rover's works in Longbridge, near Birmingham.

Labour's thwarted idealists need to be galvanised to stop the tactical unwind by promoting the nose-peg vote.

Simon Atkinson of the market research company MORI, quoted in the *Sunday Times*, April 2005.

Two major national elections within eight months of each other, in the US and Britain, brought political issues—and the means by which they are debated—under intense scrutiny in 2004/5. Guy Fawkes and the powder plotters of 1605, threatening to blow up the Houses of Parliament, found their modern counterparts in the ricin plotters and other urban terrorists whose threat to national security is foremost on the political agenda and at the hub of the **politics of fear**. A century ago in Tsarist Russia, such terrorists might well have been **sent to Siberia**; today they might be classified as **unlawful combatants** and Guantánamo Bay is the new place of exile.

Meanwhile **immigration** became a highly charged issue in the run-up to the British general election. Campaigns were launched to rid Britain of illegal Gypsy encampments, in which some newspapers notably chose the spelling 'gipsy', thereby rejecting the capital G of what is now a distinct ethnic categorization. The term **asylum seeker** was further entrenched as a replacement of the **displaced person** of the early twentieth century and as an alternative (although not synonymous) term of choice for a **refugee**.

The latter term has retained its generally neutral sense, and emphasizes both the power and the magnanimity of the provider of refuge. By contrast, 'asylum seeker' emphasizes the action of the seeker, and has been easier to provide with connotations of aggressively dodging the system. 'Asylum seeker' was the consistent term of choice in election debate, while the noun **illegals** was sometimes to be heard on the British street.

Beyond terrorism and immigration, both of which dominated the campaigns of all three major British political parties, the issues of the health service and school lunches were high on the pre-election agenda. Jamie Oliver extended the power of the celebrity chef and became an instigator of political change when the recommended average spend of authorities on each school lunch was increased as a result of his campaigning. His name entered the language as a verb with wide-ranging potential: a school could have a culinary facelift and be **Jamie Olivered**, while, thanks to the chef's liberal use of expletives on prime-time TV, 'Jamie Olivered' adjectives were invariably both spicy and raw.

To the chagrin of the newspapers, a noticeable political strategy during British electoral campaigning was the favouring of **direct communication**. Such unmediated political transaction took the form of meetings between parliamentary candidates and 'ordinary' voters, known as **drop-ins**. Some voters were pre-screened for their party allegiance and became known as **endorsers**. Meanwhile those who (together with their body parts, as in the case of the **War of Margaret's Shoulder**—see page 81) became emblems for a cause were dubbed **human shields** (see page 67), seen as part of a dubious strategy of shroud-waving and of what some critics called the climate of **New Emotionalism**.

Populist politics were equally evident in the choice of media for prime ministerial addresses. Tony Blair turned to text and email chats, daytime chat shows, and the soft sofa approach (or what some pundits called **democratic sofalism**). Doubters were dismissed by Labour's faithful as **dinner-party critics** or **shiraz quaffers** touting their **bruschetta orthodoxies**. Meanwhile, no **family**, it seemed, was mentioned without the adjective **hard-working**. Talk was of the floating **phwooaar! vote**, of **grabby** issues, and of **worm polls**. In the latter, viewers can express positive or negative reactions to a televised speech or debate using an electronic handset; as the speech progresses, their response is shown as a wavy line at the foot of the screen. In his open forums with the public, Blair was also said to have adopted a **masochism strategy**, in which he chose to face critical questioning from voters in order to restore the human face of New Labour. Such a step was deemed necessary in what was being variously dubbed the **turnout election**—voter apathy was said to be at an all-time high—and the **khaki election**, a term dating back to 1918 which links the outcome of a war with the electorate's voting decisions. Fears of **tactical unwind**, the decline of tactical voting aimed at keeping the Conservative Party out of office, were also strong.

Meanwhile, electoral fraud became a dominating theme. In Birmingham, six Labour councillors were found guilty of running the most corrupt electoral campaign in Britain for well over a hundred years. Over 3,000 postal votes were 'stolen' or amended in favour of the Labour Party, leading the British press to question the integrity of the entire election. In the verdict of the judge, the scandal of Birmingham's local election involved 'electoral fraud that would disgrace a banana republic'. **Banana republic**, a term dating back to 1935, was resurrected on several occasions in the course of subsequent election debates. **Push polling** also made the news, denoting the spreading of damaging information about opponents by telephone campaigners, often under the guise of conducting an independent survey.

Dog-whistle politics

If the Australian political guru Lynton Crosby, hired by Michael Howard to mastermind the campaigning of the Conservative Party, was said to be behind the Tories' choice of slogan 'Are you thinking what I'm thinking?'—a catchphrase from the Australian children's TV show *Bananas in Pyjamas*—he was also given credit for one of the most enduring phrases of the 2005 general election: **dog-whistle politics**.

In the same way as a high-pitched dog whistle is only audible to dogs, so dog-whistle politics is intended to rouse a specific audience without disturbing the rest of the electorate. The term appears to have originated in the US in the late 1990s, but achieved far wider currency during the Australian 2001 election thanks to a book entitled *Dog-Whistle Politics and Journalism* by Peter Manning.

There was little doubt as to the dog-whistle issues of the 2005 British election. Debates over immigration control, above all, were said to be stirring the minds of the receptive. According to the *Guardian* columnist Polly Toynbee: 'Wherever they go, the Tory "dog whistle" is stirring the dark side', referring in particular to the issue of unauthorized Gypsy encampments. Alice Thomson, writing in *The Telegraph*, linked the term to the battles between town and country over fox-hunting: 'The Tories have been blowing hard on their dog whistle and have now gathered up their hounds, but their shrill tones appear to have stopped any more voters from running to them.'

As for the Labour Party's own dog whistle, while Toynbee concluded that 'it has Crufts-loads of dogs that need calling home—but the whistle has gone missing', others identified Labour's policy for education and childcare, in which it was said to be demonstrating its **school-gate** credentials, as a **dog-whistler** of a topic.

Figurative language was evident in other areas too. The targeting of marginal seats held by the opposition became known as **decapitation**, a term originating in military use and which was high-profile during the last Iraq war. Political 'decapitation' involves the **beheading** of a party by unseating vulnerable candidates. Such use of militaristic language in political endeavour was not unique. The British election provided new examples in the form of the Conservatives' **Battle for Britain** and their warnings of government **tax bombshells**. For its part, the Labour Party announced a **demolition day** on Tory tax plans as part of their **ground war** tactics.

Remaining with figurative language, the Conservative MP Howard Flight was sacked by his party for alleging that the James review on value for money had been **sieved** to make it politically acceptable, thereby coining a new sense for 'sieve'. His party was said to be **playing dead**: declining to contradict the prospect of a Labour win with the aim of encouraging apathy on the part of Labour voters who might then stay at home on polling day. The **harvesting** of ballot papers by political canvassers for processing was known as **vote farming**, implying the treatment of potential votes as a crop and the drive for maximum returns. The hint of undue pressure was made more explicit in the term for the same process in retirement homes: **granny farming**.

Tony Blair, now the longest-serving Labour prime minister, used the extended metaphor of **marriage** to describe his relationship with the British electorate (see *Worth a Thousand Words: Images and Allusions*, pages 76–82). In his role as 'jilted' husband, Blair was clearly attempting to woo back his estranged electorate. The word **trust** became a defining one for the Labour campaign, and indeed for the Conservative camp, who encouraged the electorate to demonstrate their lack of it for the government at the booths. A further difficult relationship for the Prime Minister to manage was the one with his Chancellor, Gordon Brown. The Blair/Brown relationship was rather inevitably compared to that between Prince Charles and Camilla Parker Bowles, and the 'wedding of Tony and Gordonia' was the subject of more than one political cartoon. The rivalry between Brown and Blair, said to stem from an agreement known as **the Granita deal** (after the London restaurant in which it was said to have been struck), in which Brown allegedly agreed to let Blair stand as leader on the understanding that there would be an exchange of power at a later date, was dubbed the **Teebee Geebees**.

As well as dogs, the **elephant** also featured in the British election. Amid pre-election fever the columnist Simon Hoggart noted the appropriateness of US linguist George Lakoff's thesis *Don't Think of an Elephant*: 'Lakoff makes the point that as soon as someone tells you not to think about an elephant, you cannot get the pachyderm out of your head. In the same way, he says, the American right has brilliantly "framed" political debate so that you can't shake off the picture of the world as they see it.'

Other examples of framing cited by Lakoff are the use of such terms as **tax relief**, quickly adopted by George W. Bush in his first term in office. Add 'tax' to 'relief', Lakoff argues, and you build a metaphor which implies that taxation is an affliction, and that anybody who is against relieving this affliction is a villain. **Reform** is another word implicit in the framing of an issue for political gain. The phrase **Social Security Reform** caused a brouhaha in the US media in 2005 when the appropriateness of the word 'reform' for the President's proposed part-privatization of the social security system was widely debated. 'Reform', many argued, implies a necessary correction of something which needs mending. In the minds of many, this was not true of the system in place. As a result, alternatives such as **Social Security modification** and **Social Security revision** quickly took root.

The British Labour Party's manifesto, printed as a red pamphlet, became known as **the little red book** (even 'Chairman Blair's Little Red Book') in deliberate allusion to the little red book of quotations from Chairman Mao, perceived by the West as a weapon of mass propaganda. The Conservative Party, meanwhile, hoped to offer a **Blue Revolution**. Colours are equally strongly associated with political factions in the US. **Red** is today associated not with the left but with the right of the conservative Republicans, while a **blue state** is one which votes Democrat. A **flyover state**, meanwhile—a term which became popular during the 2000 presidential election—is one in the US heartland (and normally simply flown over by the majority of US citizens on their way to coastal cities) to which a political candidate pays a **hopscotch visit** in an effort to drum up support. That support may be **nose-holding**, a term coined in the 2004 presidential election to describe the allegiance of strongly anti-Bush voters to the Kerry campaign even while they held their noses against the 'smell' of some of its less palatable policies. The idiom was found to be just as useful during the British election campaign.

The US also had its own immigration debate. The **Minuteman Project** distilled the fears of some of a 'self-destructing America'. The original minutemen were the colonial militia in New England during the American War of Independence who organized resistance against the British military; their name came from their claim to be able to muster in one minute. The *Oxford English Dictionary* dates the figurative use of the term 'minuteman', describing someone ready to take swift action in pursuit of a cause, back to 1863. The modern Minuteman Project, a vigilante attempt to seize control of the US–Mexican border to stop illegal immigration, was seen by its participants as a grassroots effort to bring Americans to the defence of their homeland, similar to the way the original minutemen from Massachusetts did in the late 1700s. Reports that some of the 'volunteers' were carrying shotguns, and that others had illegally detained immigrants, only intensified the heat of the debate.

Four hundred years on from the Gunpowder Plot, political fireworks clearly remain a talking point.

Slogans: A short history

The political slogan is one of the most potent weapons in a party's armoury. The best linger in the public memory long after the issues driving them have moved on. The slogans of the 2005 British election were notable more for the way they failed to describe the public mood and ignite enthusiasm than for the likelihood of any lasting resonance. They also lent themselves to subversion: the Conservative slogan 'Are you thinking what I'm thinking?' became variously 'Are you sinking like we're sinking?', 'Are you smoking what we're smoking?' and 'Are you thinking? We're not' on British graffiti and on websites, and there were countless other variations.

The following is a selection of the most memorable slogans from the political campaign trail. They fall into two categories: those that advertise the strengths of the party which pitches them, and those that advertise the opponent's weaknesses. These sit alongside other, unofficial, phrases that have associated themselves with a particular election, such as **It's the economy, stupid** (see *Catchphrases through the Looking Glass*, pages 113–115) and Nancy Reagan's simple plea on her husband's behalf to **Let Reagan be Reagan**.

British general elections

1918: **Homes Fit for Heroes** (Lloyd George and the Liberal Party at the end of the First World War)

1921: **We Can Conquer Unemployment** (Lloyd George). Stanley Baldwin's Conservative Party responded with **Safety First**: in other words, no risk-taking.

1959: **Britain Belongs To You** (Labour Party)

1974: **One More Heave** (Jeremy Thorpe's Liberal Party)

1979: **Britain Isn't Working** (Conservative Party, at a time of mass unemployment under Labour)

1992: **Labour's Double Whammy** (Conservative Party, referring to "More Taxes" and "Higher Prices")

1997: **Things Can Only Get Better** (Labour Party)

2005: **Forward not back** (Labour Party). Labour were accused of poaching the line from a cartoon version of Bill Clinton in *The Simpsons*.

2005: **Vote Blair, get Brown** (Conservative Party).

2005: **Are you thinking what I'm thinking?** (Conservative Party). Tony Blair caricatured it as 'Are you remembering what I'm remembering?'

US presidential elections

1864: **Don't swap horses in the middle of a stream** (Abraham Lincoln, when the country was split by war rather than by political parties)

1884: **Ma, Ma, Where's my Pa? Gone to the White House, Ha, Ha, Ha** (James Blaine, referring to the allegedly illegitimate child that his opponent Grover Cleveland had fathered)

1900: **A Full Dinner Pail** (William McKinley, referring to the relative prosperity of his first term)

1924: **Keep Cool with Coolidge** (Calvin Coolidge)

1928: **A chicken in every pot and a car in every garage** (Herbert Hoover, claiming that he would bring prosperity to the nation)

1956: **Peace and Prosperity** (Dwight Eisenhower, in the period after the Korean War)

1964: **The stakes are too high for you to stay at home** (Lyndon B. Johnson, implying a danger of indiscriminate nuclear weapon use by his opponent Barry Goldwater if elected)

1976: **Not Just Peanuts** (Jimmy Carter, promoting qualifications beyond his job as a peanut farmer)

1984: It's morning again in America (Ronald Reagan, after the recession of the early 80s)

1992: Don't stop thinking about tomorrow (Bill Clinton, quoting from the 70s' hit song of the same name by Fleetwood Mac)

2000: Reformer with Results (George W. Bush)

2004: Let America be America again (John Kerry)

2004: Yes, America Can! (George W. Bush)

Words in the Spotlight

8

It is not only brand new words which capture the public imagination. Once in a while an older term is resurrected, or a specialized word finds wider currency, in order to articulate a new situation. In 2005, several words, phrases, and idioms moved centre stage for a period of time. Some were entirely new, while others acquired new resonance. Thanks to them, some of the key events of the year left a distinct impression on our language. The close of 2004 and the beginning of 2005 brought the word **tsunami** into dramatic relief (see page 9). Once the preserve of meteorologists and seismologists, it dominated headlines and news reports for weeks. Such was its impact that many supposed it to be a term introduced exclusively for the events in Asia: in fact the *Oxford English Dictionary* dates it back to 1897.

The following is a selection of other words which exploded onto the scene in 2005; they serve as a shorthand for the episodes which reinvigorated them.

morganatic

The marriage of Prince Charles to Camilla Parker Bowles on 9 April 2005 brought a complex legal term out of obscurity and into the arena of fierce debate. In question was whether a divorcée such as Mrs Parker Bowles would be eligible to be called Queen on Charles's succession to the throne. As the prospective union began to polarize legal and ecclesiastical commentators into camps of assent or dissent, a **morganatic** wedding was mooted as a possible solution.

Morganatic marriage was originally a German custom. It involved marriage between a high-ranking man and a woman of lower rank (rarely the other way round), in which neither the wife nor any children from the marriage were eligible to inherit the property, rank, or titles of the husband or father.

There are several famous instances of morganatic marriages. The Archduke Franz Ferdinand, whose assassination (with his wife) at Sarajevo precipitated the First World War, was married morganatically. The Mountbatten family, formerly Battenburgs, originated from the morganatic marriage of one of the sons of the Grand Duke of Hesse. The term may however be a sensitive one in British royal circles, since in November 1936 King Edward VIII proposed a morganatic marriage to Mrs Simpson, once she, like Mrs Parker Bowles, was a divorcée. The suggestion was rejected out of hand on the grounds that British law and tradition did not permit such royal marriages; hence the King's abdication.

An alternative name for 'morganatic marriage' was 'left-handed marriage', since the custom was for the husband to extend his left hand to the bride at the altar, rather than his right, as a mark of their unconventional union. In English this phrase could also at one time refer to an unmarried couple, either in an adulterous relationship or where the couple had no formal wedding: a left-handed wife was a mistress.

The etymological source of 'morganatic' is the German term *Morgengabe*, meaning 'morning gift'. The term refers to an old custom in which the husband would give a present to his wife the morning after the marriage was consummated. In a morganatic marriage such a gift would be the extent of the wife's inheritance.

In the event the royal marriage of Prince Charles was declared not to be morganatic, implying that legislation would be required to avert his new wife's automatic assumption of the title of Queen.

Degrees of consciousness

The news in March 2005 was dominated by the case of Terri Schiavo, a severely brain-damaged woman who became the centre of a tug of war which triggered extraordinary legal, congressional, and public reaction. The battle at the heart of the case pitched Terri Schiavo's parents against her husband. While Bob and Mary Schindler argued their daughter's right to be given sustenance through a feeding tube, Michael Schiavo insisted that it had been his wife's expressed wish to be allowed to die in such circumstances.

The fraught legal arguments which ensued brought two phrases from the lexicon of neuroscience into public consciousness. Together they became the unlikely turf for a war of emotions and beliefs, during which each was used as a weapon against the other side. The terms in question were **persistent vegetative state**, which most doctors and much of the US population believed Schiavo to be in, and **minimally conscious state**, which those advocating her right to live preferred. Each phrase came to define the position of the speaker towards Mrs Schiavo's condition.

In the 'minimally conscious state', which only became a diagnostic category in 2003 and which remains controversial, the suggestion is that recovery is conceivable. More importantly in the Schiavo case, it also implies that a person's awareness may extend to their condition and that therefore to let them die of starvation and dehydration is an act of cruelty. The definition of 'minimally conscious state' includes the notion of a potential transition from an 'obtunded' condition to alertness. (The term 'obtund', meaning to blunt, dull, or deaden, dates back to the seventeenth century; during the mid-nineteenth century it was completely commandeered by the medical establishment.)

A 'persistent vegetative state' is distinct from a 'permanent vegetative state'. The latter is irreversible, whereas the former implies that the sufferer is arousable, but unaware. The strange limbo of people in vegetative states poses, as the Schiavo case demonstrated, a dilemma to those who must make life-and-death decisions. Dr Wade Smith, an expert on neurocritical care, concluded that 'if two physicians sit down and examine a person like Terri Schiavo, there can be a disagreement'.

Barely a week after the death of Terri Schiavo, the decline in the health of Pope John Paul II was described in language which had similarly been the terrain of the medical profession. Towards midday on the day of his death, the Pope—already in a critical condition—had entered a **compromised state of consciousness**. The term contrasted with an earlier description of the Pope, that he was **seeing and touching Christ**.

bouncebackability

The year saw an energetic campaign for a new word to be included in future dictionaries of current English. The term **bouncebackability** was allegedly coined in 2004 by the manager of the British football club Crystal Palace, Ian Dowie, when he announced that 'Crystal Palace have shown great bouncebackability against their opponents to be really back in this game'. However, the *OED* has traced it back to at least the 1970s. The word was picked up by Sky TV's *Soccer AM* programme, who noticed its increasing frequency in post-match quotes from players and managers since Dowie's original. The programme even found an instance of use in a weather forecast, in which temperatures were said to be 'showing good bouncebackability'. A petition was subsequently launched for the word to gain inclusion in the *Concise Oxford Dictionary*. Given that two of the primary criteria applied by Oxford's lexicographers for any word to be listed in a printed dictionary are usage and durability, the widespread exposure of the term in 2005 may have given the word a good chance.

tapping up

At the same time as 'bouncebackability' was being championed, another word from the same area came into the spotlight. When the Arsenal footballer Ashley Cole was allegedly approached by rival London club Chelsea—an illegal move according to the rules of the British Premier League—he was said to have been **tapped up**. In relation to football, this phrasal verb is fairly well established in spoken language, but evidence in print is rarer.

The first citation for being 'tapped up' in the *Oxford English Dictionary* is from 1840, in the sense of being aroused or woken by tapping at the door. At around the same time, the verb was a synonym for making an arrest.

A more modern American sense exists of designating someone for a task or honour, particularly for membership of a committee or organization. Although far from conclusive, the evidence suggests that the notion of tapping someone on the shoulder, implicit in these last two senses, is behind the current use of the term within football.

hobbit

In March 2005, scientists confirmed that a creature discovered on the remote Indonesian island of Flores was most probably a new species of human. Dubbed the **hobbit** after the imaginary and tiny people of J.R.R. Tolkien's novels (who gave themselves the name, meaning 'hole-dweller'), the creature, of which the female specimen is only 3 feet tall, is thought to have lived 18,000 years ago. The new species, named *Homo floresiensis*, was discovered in October 2004 but its distinctiveness was swiftly disputed by groups who believed that the skeletons were those of pygmy humans. Detailed studies of the creature's brain (which is one third the size of the average adult human brain today) subsequently showed that it was indeed unique.

Some experts believe that the creatures were descended from a race of *Homo erectus* which came to Flores by sea and subsequently evolved into a smaller species in response to limited food supplies on the island. In this case the term 'hobbit' has developed a rather more specific sense than the figurative uses which persist today.

saviour sibling

The term **saviour sibling** featured in an October 2002 article in the *Journal of Medical Ethics*. It described a child who, through medical intervention, could be born with genetic characteristics designed to treat the illness of an existing brother or sister. The phrase belongs to the terminology of what has in recent years been called **reprogenetics**, the use of genetic techniques to control the reproductive process. It represents a specific type of **designer baby**, but while this phrase, dominant in twenty-first century headlines, implies a child customized to meet its parents' wishes, be they related to gender or appearance, a 'saviour sibling' is intended as a resource for another child.

The era of the saviour sibling began with the birth of Jamie Whitaker in 2003. His embryo had been screened to provide a genetic match for his brother Charlie, who had a fatal blood disorder. The issue came back into prominence in March 2005, when the British law lords ruled on a test case involving the creation of a saviour sibling and decreed it to be lawful.

The hotly debated topic has been explored in fiction as well as public debate: in Kazuo Ishiguro's 2005 novel *Never Let Me Go*, children are born for the purpose of becoming organ transplant donors when adult. None of the characters in the book is given a surname, reflecting perhaps their perceived incompleteness as human beings.

Like the terms used in the Terri Schiavo case, 'saviour sibling' picks up on ethical concerns related to medical and scientific development.

human shield

The term **human shield** is a good example of one of the processes of language evolution, whereby a word or phrase may make a dramatic jump from one field to another. What begins as a very conscious extension of the original then begins to take hold, until the new sense firmly coexists with the old.

The 'human shield' is a term dating back to the late nineteenth century. It describes a person or group of people placed in a potential line of fire to deter, or protect others from, an attack. The *OED* includes a citation from a *Times* article in September 1914: 'I cannot help but feel that, following the system they have inaugurated in this campaign, the Germans will use these non-combatant prisoners as human shields when they are facing the Allies.' A further sense of the term relates to the use by a criminal of a hostage to avoid capture by the police. Its point of reference has moved with circumstance: in the early 1990s 'human shield' was associated particularly with the hostages taken by Saddam Hussein in the first Gulf War.

In the spring of 2005, the focus of the term shifted again. 'Human shields on the hustings' was how the *Guardian* columnist Jackie Ashley described the use by a political party of individuals whose difficult personal circumstances exposed and ultimately symbolized shortcomings in the system. Ashley was referring to the cases of Margaret Dixon (see 'Margaret's Shoulder', page 81), and Maria Hutchings, a mother campaigning against the closure of her son's special school. Both stories were exposed by the Conservative Party, who were subsequently criticized by the government Health Minister John Reid for employing 'human shield tactics': in other words, political pawns. The metaphor proved an evocative one and received considerable attention in the press; as a result it may well survive beyond the spats of a single election.

humanzee

The word **chimera**, referring to the fabled fire-breathing monster of Greek mythology which bore a lion's head, a goat's body, and a serpent's tail, is first recorded in English in the fourteenth century in Wyclif's Bible. It is one of many animal hybrids in classical and other mythologies. Beyond its original point of reference, the word has endured in figurative language where it means 'an unreal creature of the imagination, a mere wild fancy; an unfounded conception': a sense which evolved as early as the late 1500s.

Chimeric experimentation, seen by some as the cutting edge of the biotech revolution, involves the combination of genetic material from different species, or human and animal cells, in one creature. The intention behind such research is to create animals which are similar to humans in their genetic make-up, and therefore provide more accurate models of how diseases develop. In 2005, one potential result of such experimentation was the **humanzee**, a proposed combination of human and chimpanzee material in the same organism.

The implications of producing such creatures became a matter of vociferous debate, with some critics suggesting that questions regarding its moral and legal status would throw thousands of years of ethics into chaos. With chimeric experimentation, according to the author Jeremy Rifkin in *The Guardian* (in an article entitled 'Are you a man or a mouse?'), 'scientists have the power to rewrite the evolutionary saga'.

dabbawallah

The wedding of Prince Charles to Camilla Parker Bowles brought to the public attention a term which had hitherto been largely restricted to

Mumbai (Bombay). A **dabbawallah** is a tiffin or curry carrier who brings home-cooked food to businesses. The lunch boxes are named 'dabbas', while a 'wallah' is a doer. Mumbai has an estimated 5,000 dabbawallahs, distributing almost 175,000 lunch boxes a day. The trade is over one hundred years old, and its efficiency rate—99.9% of lunches are delivered on time—has earned the dabbawallahs a six-sigma rating from *Forbes* magazine. Their developed tracking system has been studied by management institutes and gurus. Prince Charles met and talked with a group of dabbawallahs when he came to Mumbai in 2003. Two representatives were invited to the ceremony at Windsor, and brought traditional gifts of sweets called 'tilgul laddoos'.

Tartan tempters

In 2005, a new wave of romances featuring smouldering Scottish heroes became known as **plaid-rippers**, a term one step on from the **bodice-ripper** (and many on from the **bodice buttoner**). It joined a long line of inventive epithets for literary genres, dating back to the **dime novels**, **penny dreadfuls**, and **shilling shockers** of the early twentieth century.

The 1990s had brought us **lad lit** and its opposite **chick lit**, a pairing otherwise less elegantly known as **prick lit** and **clit lit**. Travel novels, meanwhile, were **trip lit**. Today there are 'lits' for all sorts of fiction types: **dad-lit** (books about fathers and children), **biker lit**, **git lit** (featuring 'yob' culture as in the style of Irvine Welsh), and **grit lit** (gritty realist novels). Historical epics (looking further back than **Vic lit**) may be known as **sword and sandals** novels, as distinct from those providing **sword and sorcery** fantasy. Many saw the unsung genre of the twentieth century as being the **sex-and-shopping** (or **S and F**, for 'shopping and fucking') novel, not to be confused with the lighter **bonkbuster**, a genre preceded (in a purer fashion) by stories under the **Mills and Boon** imprint which dates back to 1912, and which has become a label in itself.

Those detective stories with a traditional, often British and rural, setting and a lady detective are now fondly known as **cosies**, a term reminiscent of the **Aga saga**. By contrast, if dealing with gritty urban themes, they can be **hard-boiled**. These sit alongside the categories of **TOT** stories ('Triumph Over Tragedy'), and **HIBK** ('Had I but known what I know now...', a term coined by Ogden Nash), **fem-jep** ('female in jeopardy'), and **WIP** ('Women In Peril') fiction.

All of which suggest that creative wordplay is as useful in descriptions of fiction as in its contents.

Showing Your Label: Language on the Social Ladder

9

I thought everyone must know that a *short* jacket is always worn with a silk hat at a private view in the morning.

Edward VII to Sir Frederick Ponsonby (who was wearing a tailcoat).

Very short hair and souped-up Vauxhall Novas are chav, as is functional illiteracy, a burgeoning career in petty crime and the wearing of one's mobile telephone around the neck. . . . A teenage single mum chewing gum or drawing on a cigarette as she pushes her baby, Keanu, to McDonald's to meet the chav she believes to be his father is a chavette.

Neil Tweedie in *The Times*, December 2004.

You used to define yourself as a mod or a punk; now all the kids seem to want to look the same. I've got a lot of admiration for the Goths. At least they make the effort.

Steve Mason, of the Scottish experimentalist group *The Beta Band*, 2005.

Will the people in the cheaper seats clap your hands? All the rest of you, if you'll just rattle your jewellery.

John Lennon to the audience at the Royal Variety Performance in 1964.

Every year there emerges a handful of new words which make a dramatic impact on many levels. The most prominent among them point to how society is evolving. In 2004, the word **chav** was used to describe everything from an individual to an entire social class. The force with which it entered our daily vocabulary, and the intense debate surrounding it, provided an example of how the vocabulary of fashion can be as much a tool of social categorization as the clothes it describes.

The term 'chav' was not new. As far as etymologists can tell, it derives from a nineteenth-century Romany word *chavi*, meaning child. Largely confined in its geographical spread to Kent (and in particular to Chatham), it has survived as a term meaning 'mate' both amongst school-children and in distinct circles such as the building trade. In 2004 it took on more unpleasant connotations when it became a pejorative social label for a white, urban underclass: those said to sport 'council house chic' and to be demonstrably lacking in both education and taste. Newspapers— broadsheets and tabloids alike—launched national debates about the term's legitimacy, and few were tongue-in-cheek. While the reliably strident commentator Julie Burchill empathized with the 'chav', denouncing the 'moribund middle classes' for their 'chippiness and envy', the *Daily Mail* declared: 'They're white, they're dumb, they're vulgar.' From its apparently benign beginnings, 'chav' became the expression of the acrimony in the British class system.

While the status of the 'chavs' or **chavsters** attracted polarized views, their fashion appeared more straightforward. The dress code: **flash trash**, consisting of pristine white trainers, baseball caps, the (sometimes imitation) Burberry check, flashy jewellery, and what was seen as a general lack of taste. Celebrities became the victims of **chavspotting** on account of their tastes, and were consequently lampooned if found sufficiently **chavvish**. Meanwhile, fashion houses began to debate the likelihood of 'chav' wardrobes becoming perversely desirable and thus whether to align themselves with the new phenomenon.

The term 'chav' joined a fairly long list of others of the same kind, including **white trash**, **trailer trash**, **redneck**, and **hillbilly**. Most make some reference, tacit or otherwise, to ethnicity as well as lifestyle, but they are nonetheless generally seen as examples of class, rather than racial, prejudice. (The term **pikey** started out as a derogatory term for a Gypsy, a now recognized distinct ethnic group, but is now used more generally to mean a lout.) Yet if the term 'chav' was generally agreed to be derogatory, it was also the view of some commentators that those who 'earned' it were legitimate targets because they were white. In other words, criticism of the average 'chav' could not be deemed to be racist in the traditional sense;

rather it was an example of social racism. In *The Making of London's White Trash*, Michael Collins tells of a woman who, at a media party, complained that having moved to London's Elephant and Castle, she could not source aubergines locally. She described the area as 'very white', and made it clear that her neighbours were not the kind she was looking for. 'Her multiculturalism made her colourless,' writes Collins, '[but] her class made her superior.'

Bling bling, and the entire 'bling' lexicon, which includes **blingy**, **blingers**, and **blinging it up**, provides a further example of the links between fashion and the social scale.

Despite being recorded in print for the first time in 1999, in a song by the US rapper B.G., 'bling' really hit the public radar in the early 2000s, when it was used as shorthand for anything ostentatious and over-materialistic. Etymologically, the term is most likely to have been coined as a representation of light reflecting off a diamond, or of the sound of flashy jewellery clanging together. Although ultimately it has been applied across gender, race, and class, in its beginnings 'bling' was almost exclusively used in reference to black culture, firstly within it, and then as a description of it. It emerged as an offshoot of 'gangsta rap' within hip-hop culture; for some 'bling-bling' hip-hop promoted the stereotypes of criminality, material worship, and envy which black culture had sought to eradicate. As the term progressed, its roots were diluted to the extent that 'bling' became more a descriptor of fashion than of ethnicity. Nonetheless, its core associations with black culture are not completely lost, in the same way as 'chav' is unlikely to stray far from its white point of reference. Writing in *The Times* about black style, Bonnie Greer puts it thus: 'Bling is all about competition, or "the dozens" as it is called in the US: in other words, one-upmanship with style.'

The repercussions of the 'chav' debate are likely to be felt for a while to come. As a social label, however, it has a fairly large number of precedents, including some which date back as far as the eighteenth century.

In 1785, Grose's *Dictionary of the Vulgar Tongue* included the entry **Whitechapel** as the name of a social 'breed', defining those within it as 'fat, ragged, and saucy'. A 'Whitechapel beau' was described in the same work as someone 'who dresses with a needle and thread, and who undresses with a knife'. The *Oxford English Dictionary* includes a citation which goes back even further, to 1700, when a 'White-chappel portion' consisted of 'two torn Smocks, and what Nature gave'.

Whitechapel, in the East End of London, was for a long time one of the poorer districts of the city, infamous from the late nineteenth century for its link with Jack the Ripper. Later, other terms such as **shawlie** (1914) emerged, denoting a poor working-class woman, traditionally from Ireland and typically wearing a shawl. A century on, Essex became the new focus of class derision; the term **Essex girl** resonating with labels such as **Mondeo Man** and **white van man**. At the other end of the social scale, the **Sloane Rangers**, 'girls in pearls' known for their Lady Di haircuts (women), and Barbour jackets, corduroys, and striped shirts (men), became a defining term of the eighties, geographically based in the moneyed and upper-class Sloane Street of London's Chelsea. In 2005, **Chelsea tractor** looks likely to take root as the term for the four-by-four vehicles driven by well-heeled **yummy mummies**.

The 1960s in Britain saw violent clashes between two groups who categorized themselves by their clothes as much as their politics. **Mods**— clean-cut and neat, sporting Italian leather shoes and riding Italian scooters—were pitched against the **Rockers**, who prided themselves on their masculine scruffiness and their biker culture. In this sense, the hostility between the two groups was explicitly aesthetic. Their respective social groups, ironically, were not far away from each other: like **punk rockers** of the late 1970s and early 1980s, and the **Teddy boys** of the 1950s, both represented disaffected youth. Today the teenage social scene finds expression in the fashions of **grungers**, **skaters**, and **goths**, who in turn do battle with **townies** and **neds**. While each group has its own distinct fashion and accessories, its members all mark the desire to be different from the perceived norms of the rest of society, and are conformist in their adoption of the group's uniform. As Alice Cooper put it for the rockers of the 1970s: 'The hippies wanted peace and love. We wanted Ferraris, blondes, and switchblades.'

In the Netherlands, the British sportswear label Lonsdale faced bans in 2005 after racist gangs appropriated the brand, sporting jackets strategically placed over the top of a Lonsdale sweatshirt to leave only the letters NSDA visible, the acronym for the *Nationalsozialistische Deutsche Arbeiterpartei* (the National Socialist Party). Thus **Lonsdale youth** became a term for teenagers with extreme right-wing tendencies.

Entire fashion labels can become emblematic of a social class as well as a political viewpoint. The company Burberry, famous for its Burberry check, saw its sales plummet as a result of the media's insistence on its links with 'chavs'. In 2005 it regained ascendancy when Camilla Parker Bowles pronounced Christopher Bailey, one of its designers, to be her favourite, and Burberry became a key ingredient of **Camilla chic**. The twists and turns in the Burberry story show both the vulnerability of fashion to social categorization, and its resilient ability to renew itself through reassociation. The term 'dress code' really does have meaning.

Worth a Thousand Words: Images and Allusions

10

Sir, I was sorry to read that the Grand National-winning jockey Graham Lee has been side-lined with worrying injuries: 'This is the first time I've broken the left collarbone...it will come right quickly, given time, but I certainly need to be riding again early next week, to get my eye back in.'

> Letter to the Editor, headed 'Blinkers On', in *The Times*, 6 March 2005.

As far as the public and the press were concerned, preferring Parker Bowles to his wife was like paying for jellied eels when the lobster thermidor was free.

> Allison Pearson on Prince Charles, *Sunday Times*, February 2005.

I'd better court him. It is better to be riding the tiger's back than let it rip your throat out.

> Tony Blair's words, on courting Rupert Murdoch, as recalled by former editor of *The Mirror* Piers Morgan.

Canadians see him as a sorcerer's apprentice leading the US and the world over a cliff.

> A mixed metaphor attributed to Canadian pollster Frank Graves, speaking of the 'somewhat irrational demonization' of George Bush.

I spend my life being Odysseus. I tie myself to the mast, and I don't listen to the Sirens.

> Disney chief executive Michael Eisner. Among the Sirens he listed were investment bankers and the media.

Figurative language is language which extends the literal; it uses the image to appeal to the imagination. The successful image is one packed with resonances which are left unspoken, but which the listener or reader will immediately process. Allusions, metaphors, similes, and personifications are all components in this form of linguistic shorthand.

2005 provided numerous illustrations of figurative language at its most effective (although not always popular). One of its most prominent examples originated in the rhetoric surrounding the Iraq war. If the real **weapons of mass destruction** were never found, allusions to them sprang up everywhere, often in startling contexts. The phrase, which has shown considerable longevity, continues to be played upon with relish. Journalists have found figurative relevance in subjects as diverse as football battles and Page Three girls, sporting their 'weapons of mass affection'. This last example of transference had numerous outings. The Advertising Standards Authority received hundreds of complaints over an advertisement placed by the airline company Easyjet which featured a picture of a woman's breasts in a bikini top and the claim of offering the 'lowest fares to the sun'. Above the picture the ad's slogan read: 'Discover weapons of mass destruction'. Flippant as these uses may have been, the strength of the original context was never lost: the allusive power of the phrase lies in the context of something whose existence was never discovered.

Not surprisingly, 2005 was also a year rich in the use of allusions within the political arena. In the run-up to the general election, the shadow of the phrase **something of the night** hovered over the Leader of the Opposition Michael Howard. Ann Widdecombe's famous description of her colleague in May 1997, in the aftermath of the Tory election defeat and John Major's resignation, was said at the time to have derailed Howard's chances of becoming party leader. In a memorable article from *The Guardian* in March 2005, the critic and commentator Mark Lawson wrote of 'Mike Lite's new light and smiley style'. So marked was Howard's transformation that 'he had something of the bright about him'. (Clearly unconvinced, Lawson also included the wry simile that 'confronted by first-time voters, Howard sounded like an elderly vicar trying to get down with the kids'.) In the same newspaper, columnist Polly Toynbee picked up another in a whole string of associations attached to Michael Howard: this time that of a vampire, an image born out of Howard's family history and his father's birthplace in northern Transylvania. Writing of the 'cheek of the Tory campaign...believing they are at last free of their past', Toynbee declared that 'Old something-of-the-night has escaped his coffin: the Dracula joke is even a little cuddly.' Howard himself was bemused by the wealth of allusive references he attracted: 'So far this year they've compared me to Fagin, Shylock, and flying pigs. This morning Peter Hain even called me a mongrel' (see page 110).

As the Tory leader discovered, certain images are difficult to shake off. Gerald Ratner was once best known as the head of a highly successful high-street chain of jewellers. When, in 1991 and with intentional irony, he referred to his merchandise as 'crap', he was forced to resign and the share price of his former company plummeted. At the same time, the phrase **doing a Ratner** entered the English language as an allusion to commercial hubris. Until 2005, the name of the doyenne of British cookery Delia Smith reflected a reputation very different to that of Ratner. **Doing a Delia** had even been recorded in some dictionaries, meaning simply to prepare a dish which follows one of Smith's recipes. An episode at a football match between Chelsea and Norwich City (the latter being the team in which she is the major shareholder) may, however, shift the allusive significance of the phrase. Forgetting the presence of live TV cameras, and with the aim of stirring up support for the languishing team, Smith grabbed a microphone and shouted, 'We need a twelfth man here. Where are you? Let's be having you. Come on!' Her rallying cry was replayed both on news bulletins and the Internet, while Delia T-shirts were rushed out, printed with the slogan 'Letsby Avenue'.

Celebrity shorthand is not a new linguistic phenomenon, and it is one which by its nature is self-renewing as personalities come and go. Media exposure, and in particular the sound-bite headline, almost guarantees that individuals become known for a single attribute and so begin to be used allusively. In a *Times* article during the run-up to Gordon Brown's spring 2005 budget, the chief leader-writer Tim Hames variously characterized the Chancellor as **Capability Brown**, the **Carol Vorderman of the Exchequer** ('numbers will be hurled at MPs'), and 'the **Martha Stewart of politics**—all the richer for a period of relative confinement'.

Beyond words, visual images can cluster around particular figures, acquiring allusive resonance. The political and moral stand taken by Martin Bell, the well-known war reporter who successfully stood against Neil Hamilton in the Tatton by-election in the wake of the 'cash for questions' scandal, came to be symbolized by his favoured white suit. The suit symbolized his clean reputation in the midst of the 'sleaze' era. When Neil Hamilton and his wife, Christine, were later given their own chat show, Christine famously said of Bell: 'I don't want his white suit anywhere near my red sofa.' Since then, **white suit** has come to be used as both a noun and an adjective (as in 'white-suit candidate'), each functioning as a simple shorthand for honest politics. 'Who will fill the white suit?' asked a *Guardian* article, which explored the role of the political maverick and the possibility of a Bell-style challenge to Tony Blair's seat in Sedgefield in the 2005 general election. The word 'candidate' itself (like the word 'candid') comes from the Latin word meaning 'white': a person seeking office in Roman times traditionally wore a white toga.

The name of a dramatic event in history can carry the full allusive force of the event itself (see *The Language of Events*, pages 5–10). In March 2005 the *New York Times* carried a piece headed **The Beirut Tea Party**, which quoted a Lebanese political analyst Nawaf Salam saying of the recent pro-democracy demonstrations in Lebanon: 'It was our Boston Tea Party.' The speaker did not need to say more: the comparison drawn with a historical event which galvanized patriots into resistance was clear enough, thanks to the strength of the image. The same is true of the series of so-called **Colour Revolutions**—**Cedar**, **Orange**, **Yellow**, and **Tulip**—all of which draw on the original Czech (bloodless) **Velvet Revolution**. The first three terms refer to the popular uprisings in Lebanon, Ukraine, and Kyrgyzstan respectively; cedar is the national emblem of Lebanon, while the colours are those adopted by the revolutionaries as their symbol. The tulip image was used in allusion to the **Rose Revolution** of Georgia in 2003, in which officers of the government held roses in their hands.

In the case of allusions such as these, the contextual resonance matters more than who said it. Metaphorical language often originates in a link to a specific event. The metaphor of the **tsunami**, for example, was used in numerous contexts in 2005 following the Asian disaster in December 2004. At the annual summit of the World Economic Forum, the French

President Jacques Chirac spoke of the threat of 'silent tsunamis' of despair, infectious diseases, and famine, while 'tsunami' replaced 'deluge' in many descriptions of protest and support.

Metaphors such as that of the tsunami are often quickly absorbed into general language and, like quotations, can be reused as powerful descriptors of subsequent events. In his speech at the inauguration of his second term of presidency, George W. Bush invoked the imagery of fire to emphasize his determination to win the 'war on terror': '**We have lit a fire in the minds of men**. It warms those who feel its power, it burns those who fight its progress, and one day this untamed fire of freedom will reach the darkest corners of our world.' Much of Bush's speech to the Capitol was couched in religious language, and his imagery had resonances of Moses leading God's chosen people to the Promised Land, following a pillar of fire. Bush's words were dubbed the **Burning Bush** speech: alluding to the Biblical image of the bush that burned but was not consumed. The phrase 'lit a fire in the minds of men' has its origins in Dostoevsky's nineteenth-century novel *The Devils*, which charts the ineffectual efforts of a group of terrorists to bring down a tyrannical tsarist regime. One of the characters declares the futility of trying to put out a fire started by the terrorists: 'The fire is in the minds of men and not in the roofs of the houses.' Commentators such as *The Guardian*'s James Meek were bemused as to whether the President was 'identifying with the terrorists—or the tyrants'. It is quite likely that Bush borrowed a figure of speech without realizing the full extent of the reference.

The extended metaphor is often at home in political life. Tony Blair's desire to appeal to the female electorate in the pre-election months was said to have found voice in his use of the metaphor of marriage. In his speech at Labour's spring conference, the Prime Minister compared his relationship with the people of Britain to a marriage in difficulty. 'And before you know it you raise your voice. I raise mine. Some of you throw a bit of crockery.... Now you, the British people, have to sit down and decide whether you want the relationship to continue.' Some commentators saw in Blair's words a calculated femininity and emotionalism: part of a bid to counterbalance the perceived 'macho' politics of his cabinet. Certainly his image echoed a much earlier quote from Saki, the early twentieth-century short-story writer, which linked premiers and the married state: 'We all know that Prime Ministers are wedded to the truth, but like other married couples they sometimes live apart' (*The Unbearable Bassington*, 1912).

Body politics

Political catchphrases are also frequently laden with resonances. None more so, perhaps, than those involving 'dog-whistle issues': those issues which appeal to certain types of voter and which become focal points at election time. In 2005 the **War of Margaret's Shoulder** was the latest step in a line of such issues encapsulated in a single allusive frame. As each of the British political parties fought for electoral advantage over the running of the National Health Service, the case of Margaret Dixon—whose shoulder operation had apparently been cancelled seven times—was seized upon as a symbol of a failing system. The use of a single image based on an individual story was reminiscent of previous campaign confrontations. What each of them has in common is the metonymic use of the part to stand for the whole.

In 2002 it was the **War of Rose's Socks** which was high on the Conservative political agenda. Nurses at London's Whittington Hospital were accused of failing to change 94-year-old Rose Addis's bloodstained socks while she languished in a casualty side ward for three days. Ten years earlier, a key issue of the 1992 British election was the **War of Jennifer's Ear**, a story similar to that of 'Margaret's Shoulder' and in which a young girl was facing long delays in her operation for glue ear. On that occasion it was the Labour Party who hoped to use the story to shore up its lead on the issue of health over the incumbent Conservative government.

The label 'Jennifer's Ear' was itself a deliberate echo of a much earlier case of a political pawn, dating back to 1739. The **War of Jenkins' Ear** was a prelude to the War of Austrian Succession which pitted the British and their American colonists against Spain. The war was named after Robert Jenkins, captain of the ship *Rebecca*, who claimed Spanish guards had cut off his ear in 1731.

He exhibited the ear in the British House of Commons, inflaming public opinion against the Spanish. The government of the British Prime Minister Robert Walpole reluctantly declared war on 23 October 1739.

In its requirement of a shared knowledge, figurative language can function as a code between the initiated, much as slang does among the young. The verbal images most likely to entrench themselves in the language are those which have resonance for the wider cross-section of the population.

11

The four-letter shower should be coming out the mouths of provocateurs on some sort of crusade to radically reconfigure the cultural landscape, not chefs looking to sell chunky books.

Paul Morley in *The Guardian*, March 2005.

Punk really is dead: the former Sex Pistol Glen Matlock now minds the bollocks.

Guardian article, March 2005, reporting that Glen Matlock, former member of the Sex Pistols band which once infamously used the word 'fuck' repeatedly on live television, now objects to strong language in modern society.

The Everly Brothers once sang 'Only trouble is, gee-whizz, I'm dreaming my life away'. So much more poetic than 'I'm wasting my f***ing time'.

Sunday Times Style magazine, April 2005.

Now fuck off and cover something important you twats.

Alastair Campbell in an email sent in error to a reporter on the political programme *Newsnight*, February 2005. The former Director of Communications for the Labour Party said in a follow-up email that the recipient should 'see the funny side'.

In 2005 swearing once again became a talking point. The year which saw an advertisement for the Jeep Cherokee with the slogan 'Jeep: The Original Dirty Four-Letter Word' also marked the twentieth anniversary of the first use of the word 'fuck' on British television. It further produced the screening of a programme which attracted an unprecedented number of complaints in the history of its broadcaster. For many, the years between these events have seen a dramatic shift in our attitude towards obscenity on the public stage; for others, the second was simply a continuum of the first. Who is right? Have we relaxed our morals to the extent that swearing is now a normal part of public life, or have our taboos simply changed?

In November 1965 the critic Kenneth Tynan voiced an expletive on a late-night programme and provoked moral outrage and parliamentary indignation. 'I doubt,' he said, 'there are very many rational people in this world to whom the word "fuck" is particularly diabolical or revolting or totally forbidden.' Tynan's confidence was ill-judged; beyond his own 'rational' circle were many who disapproved, some passionately. Four separate motions censuring him were tabled in the House of Commons, while the morality campaigner Mary Whitehouse wrote a letter to the Queen, expressing her view that 'Tynan ought to have his bottom smacked'.

In January 2005, the BBC broadcast a live screening of *Jerry Springer, the Opera*, an irreverent take on the world of the controversial chat-show host. Over 15,000 complaints were made to the public service broadcaster even before transmission. On the day after the programme was shown, *The Sun* newspaper announced that it had counted 3,168 uses of the 'f-word' and 297 uses of the 'c-word', on what it termed 'just another night on the BBC'.

Rival newspapers, such as the liberal-minded *Guardian*, lost no time in pointing out some of the other stories making *The Sun*'s headlines on the same day, including 'I had sex with chatline girl—and her boyfriend'. Yet while the broadsheet printed out the words 'fuck' and 'cunt' in full in its description of *Jerry Springer*, the tabloid avoided 'full-frontal vowels and consonants' by using asterisks or by restricting its transcription to the initial letter. The same divide was evident in the reporting of the alleged insult from one of John Reid's supporters against *Newsnight* presenter Jeremy Paxman (in the wake of Paxman's comment that the Health Secretary was an 'attack dog': see page 109–110): some papers reported that Paxman had been called a 'wanker', while others preferred 'w****r'.

For a serious broadsheet to opt for the full obscenity rather than a sanitized version is perhaps not surprising. *The Guardian*'s profile is of a radical, free-thinking newspaper uninhibited by bourgeois shibboleths. Neither need it be ironic that a tabloid such as *The Sun* is more reticent in such matters. The paper aligns itself with what it perceives to be the majority view: namely that, while scandals and sensations are of public interest, uncensored obscenity is not.

The history of the reporting of taboo words in the press is enlightening. The *Oxford English Dictionary*, the first edition of which (published between 1884 and 1928) included entries for neither *fuck* nor *cunt*, did nevertheless give a 1927 citation from the *Saturday Review of Literature* which speaks of 'all nine of the tabooed Anglo-Saxon monosyllables'. During the Watergate inquiry, the term 'expletive deleted' became the infamous and frequent editorial amendment of transcripts of Richard Nixon's presidential conversations. The conventional use of asterisks in journalism to indicate excised letters is in fact a fairly recent development. From the eighteenth century up until at least the middle of the twentieth century, the convention was to have a single solid line between the first and last letters of the offending word, or alternatively to show the first letter only. In an article responding to readers' complaints and queries over *The Guardian*'s use of strong language, the readers' editor Ian Mayes quotes one correspondent on the use of asterisks: 'Every reader merely substitutes the correct letters and the offensiveness of the sentence remains intact. It seems coy to suppose otherwise.' This particular objection is shared by many, who believe that by including asterisks the tabloids draw greater attention to the word they are apparently suppressing. The link between sensationalism and censorship is a close one, as the success of chart singles banned from the airwaves because of perceived blasphemy or obscenity amply demonstrates.

In their attitude towards swearing and taboo language, the British press is markedly less prudish than its US counterpart. A new puritanism seems to be emerging in the US, where tight editorial control is fully evident in the frequency with which words with the potential to offend are bleeped out. As a result, US radio and television, strongly influenced by the advertisers who fund them, are largely either clean or cleaned up, and the shows of 'shock jocks' are particularly scrutinized. The Federal Communications Commission, which monitors America's publicly-owned airways, reprimanded the channel NBC for airing *U2*'s Bono saying 'fucking brilliant' at the 2003 Golden Globe Awards; the FCC's standards are supposedly governed by 'contemporary community broadcast standards'.

Even stronger models of control exist elsewhere in the world. In Belgorod, 450 miles southwest of Moscow, a woman was arrested in 2005 for swearing in a public place. Her punishment—a fine with the possibility of imprisonment if she were to reoffend—was part of an unusual experiment aimed at purging the Russian language of obscenities. Ads urging people to express themselves without resorting to swearing were run on TV and radio, while a poster featuring a man with his tongue cut out by a pair of shears carried a slogan which translates as 'Your tongue is your enemy. Swearing is the death of your soul.'

Britain is not without its own examples of pushing the boundaries of acceptable taste. Programmes featuring celebrity chefs such as Jamie Oliver and Gordon Ramsay, in their suggestion that swearing is crucial to culinary creativity, are often noted as much for their language as for their recipes. Oliver's success in securing greater investment in British school meals (following his TV series *School Dinners*, in which fruity language was the order of the day) was celebrated in a *Times* cartoon by Peter Brookes in which Tony Blair is seen trying on the latest in a line of masks. The Prime Minister's speech bubble reads: 'Er...Think I'll be Jamie F*@*@ Oliver today!' Such satire betrays the degree to which swearing can irritate as well as offend: one result was the creation of the term 'chefiquette' for a backlash movement to preserve decency in both language and behaviour in professional kitchens.

Tynan's use of the word 'fuck' was ahead of its time. Today, it seems to be ubiquitous. 'Fuck' is a multi-purpose expletive. It can be used to deliver humour, irony, sarcasm, anger, or violence. So common is it on British television (after the watershed set for it; 'cunt' has another, later, schedule watershed), that in 2004 the British Board of Film Classification began a survey to establish its acceptability among children. It is worth bearing in mind however that the increase in swearing in the media may be a result of changes in the formality of television and radio, which have become places of demotic speech in a way they never used to be. Rather than a relaxation of morals, it may be this informality which is directing our standards. School dictionaries reflect the other side of the picture: they do not include words such as 'fuck' or 'cunt', while obscenity filters on the computer networks of many publicly-funded institutions are the norm.

Clearly some swear words are diluted in their capacity to shock over time. Prince Charles's whispered comment to his sons about journalists—'bloody people'—inadvertently picked up on a microphone during a Royal press call, seems positively restrained and old-fashioned today, yet when 'bloody' was first used on stage in 1916, during George Bernard Shaw's *Pygmalion*, it caused a sensation. The word 'fuck', however, clearly retains a shock value, even if it is not what it once was. Without it, the FCUK campaign of the clothes company French Connection, and the text messages sent to young voters in Labour's 2001 election campaign ('Cldn't give a XXXX for lst ordrs? Then vote Labour for extra time'), would have been redundant. The latter example played on the memorable ad slogan for the Australian Castlemaine 4X beer advertising campaign, 'Couldn't give a XXXX for anything else'. The advertising campaign drew on a stereotype of Australian rednecks and their fondness for swearing.

Similarly, the euphemisms which have been created around 'fuck' would not have thrived were their diluting effect not required. Yet whether they do provide a soft focus is debatable: perhaps because they share the same plosive force of the 'f' sound, alternatives such as 'frigging' are not far below 'fuck' in their expletive power. Similarly, 'kinell'—a contraction of 'fucking hell'—was an alternative but not entirely euphemistic sidestep in the 90s. (Meanwhile 'fugly', = 'fucking ugly/fuck ugly', is on the ascendant: see page 12.) This flirting with taboos suggests that the taboos themselves are intact.

The word 'cunt' has undoubtedly retained a stronger shock value than 'fuck'. The intention behind current examples of use, including the name of the pop band *Selfish Cunt*—invariably printed in full in the music press—is almost always to provoke rather than to fit in. Today there is evidence of 'cunt' giving rise to adjectives, possibly as a stronger alternative to 'fucking': Oxford's language databases have examples of both 'cunting' and 'cuntish'.

In 2005 *The Guardian* reported that 'playground taunts such as "slut" and "your mum's a whore" will be going the way of hopscotch and spinning tops, as schools begin cracking down on swear words'. The article followed a move by the National Union of Teachers to draw up a list of 'words... [that] promote the attitude that females are lesser beings, and as lesser beings they can become the target of violence'. Such debate throws an interesting light on the links between insult and perceptions of personal honour. Some terms of abuse have remained constant over time: 'son-of-a-bitch', for example, dates back to the fourteenth century. It is famously used by the character of Edmund in Shakespeare's *King Lear*, who describes the fate of illegitimacy as 'nothing but the composition of a knave, beggar, coward, pandar, and the son and heir of a mongrel bitch'. Today the term retains its sting, even as illegitimacy has become accepted.

Insults regarding sexual slander, such as those above denounced by the NUT, have also endured. The use of **slag**, to describe a promiscuous woman or 'slattern', dates back to the eighteenth century and originates in the sense of the noun as 'refuse matter'; it has lost little of its power in two hundred years.

One of the central tenets of swearing is that the force of any given obscenity depends heavily on the intention of the speaker. Words such as 'fuck', 'bugger', and 'bastard' can be used as terms of affection ('you daft old bugger') as well as of offence. Recently terms of abuse such as 'nigger', 'Paki', and 'queer' have been reclaimed by those within the communities against which they were used, although their benign status remains restricted to them: in the wider community they are considered as offensive as before.

Perhaps one of the most telling aspects of modern swearing is that the majority of its lexicon has been around for years, even centuries. 'Fuck' has been considered taboo since its written appearance in the sixteenth century, while 'cunt' dates back to the early thirteenth century where it appears to have been recorded as part of the London street name 'gropecuntlane' before transmuting into a term for female genitals and then into a term of abuse. The similes of swearing 'like a trooper', 'like a fishmonger's wife', and 'like a sailor' have likewise stood still, and show little sign of being replaced in any consistent or permanent way. Today's freedom of speech means that we have the opportunity to change our profanities as often as we change our general vocabulary; yet for the most part we keep to the old. The fact that we encounter them with unprecedented frequency appears not to have shaken off their power. In spite of appearances, our taboos seem to be reasonably secure.

Oncoming Priority:
British English in the US

12

She may or may not keep her legs crossed in the remake, as she is getting well past her sell-by date.

Ministers and Shin Bet director Avi Dichter discussed how to deal with the Israeli far-right in the run-up to the Gaza withdrawal.

The tapes went missing during shipment to an undisclosed data-storage facility for safekeeping.

President Clinton deserves full marks for putting three top warriors who care about people and want to do the right thing in charge of the Air Force.

All of the above quotations are extracts from American newspapers. They share one common and surprising element, namely that each contains a Briticism (**sell-by date**, **run-up**, **went missing**, **full marks**) that has recently attained enough currency in American English to be no longer considered remarkable or jarring to readers and listeners.

In April 2005 Timothy Kenny, a professor of journalism at the University of Connecticut, wrote in the *LA Times* of 'a virus that's infecting American media these days: Britspeak'. So, he writes, Americans **send up** instead of 'parody', and their thoughts reach a **full stop** instead of merely ending. A correct answer is **spot on** rather than 'dead on'. Further causes for lament included **queueing up** rather than 'standing in line', **sacked** for 'fired', and (also the bête noire of many Britons) **at the end of the day** instead of 'in the end'.

Kenny expressed despair at what he perceived to be 'a cottage industry in some quarters'. Of course, its counterpart, the absorption into British English of Americanisms, has a long—and for some, regrettable—history. From the beginning, the general assumption has been that American-bred vocabulary is by its very nature inferior. Complaints by the British media of new and unfortunate American usages that have slipped into the stream of national discourse are commonplace. As long ago as 1935, the BBC correspondent Alistair Cooke, famed for his weekly broadcasts of *Letters from America*, was remarking that the average Briton uses dozens of Americanisms every day.

By contrast, the appearance of a new Briticism in American English was, until recently, a much rarer phenomenon. In 2001, the *New York Times* devoted an entire article to the fact that **bespoke**, in the context of computer technology, had gained a foothold in American English, despite coming from across the water.

Today, Americans have the opportunity of hearing and reading more British English than ever before, thanks to satellite broadcasting, the Internet, classic British comedies such as *Fawlty Towers* and *Monty Python*, and the globalization of the news industry. A further, backdoor, channel for some of the Briticisms that penetrate the American vernacular is provided by journalists based abroad. Many turns of phrase that were previously rare in American English have now come into the discourse of American correspondents abroad. These are then heard in their broadcasts sent home before finally settling down into the vocabulary of those who hear them.

In the sentences above: *sell-by date*, a term which is now established in both UK and US English, is a highly successful Briticism. The US equivalents were formerly *pull date* and *expiration date*, neither of which gives the immediacy of the British version. Today, particularly in figurative uses, *sell-by date* is the term of choice. Until the adoption of *run-up*, the US English lexicon provided no single word to characterize the period leading up to something. Similarly, things in America have only recently begun to *go missing*, albeit with an added edge: the notion that, when something *goes missing*, things are not where they should be for suspect reasons, is slightly stronger in US English. Finally, whereas previously Americans would hand out good or bad *report cards*, and give passing or failing *grades*, they now give *marks* and *full marks* as well.

Those who regard British as the purest form of English might hope that it finally regains the upper hand and becomes the model and authority it set out to be when it crossed the ocean 400 years ago. Such an outcome, however, is unlikely, as the decision to produce an American English 'translation' of the *Harry Potter* series would suggest. In J. K. Rowling's books, terms such as *gormless, nutter, sherbet lemon, Sellotape, bobble hat, jelly, crumpets,* and *quits* were all considered obscure for the US market, as were idioms such as *pop my clogs* (changed to 'kick the bucket') and to *grass on* ('squeal on'), and names such as *Adalbert Waffling* (which became 'Bathilda Bagshot'). All of these changes were to the consternation of many hardened Potter fans who made the British edition a hotly prized item.

It is perhaps not surprising that the strength of the political alliance between the US and Britain is likely to be echoed in linguistic behaviour. The current trend looks set to continue, and Americans may well be more inclined than at any time in the last few centuries to let Briticisms find root in American soil. English now flies across the ocean in both directions, via dozens of media, and in volumes unprecedented at any time in history. For British English viewed from its homeland, the situation is perhaps similar to standing in front of a 'Give Way'—or what in the US is called an 'Oncoming Priority'—sign: the passage accommodates travel in both directions, but the right of way belongs to traffic coming from the opposite direction.

For Better or Worse: Our Changing Usage

13

As far as I'm concerned, 'whom' is a word that was invented to make everyone sound like a butler.
> Calvin Trillin in *The Nation*, 1985.

Language is more fashion than science, and matters of usage, spelling and pronunciation tend to wander around like hemlines.
> Bill Bryson in *The Independent*, 1994.

From now until May 5, me and my colleagues will be out every day in every part of Britain...
> Tony Blair, announcing the date of the 2005 British general election to the waiting press outside Number 10, and using the wrong pronoun ('me' rather than 'I').

Fifty years ago, Paul Berg recorded in his *Dictionary of New Words in English* some of the terms which were becoming bugbears of the language purist. They included **underprivileged**, **decontaminate**, **finalize**, **genocide**, and **infrastructure**.

It is a measure of our language's persistence that every one of these words is used today without question or scruple. What was once labelled incorrect is now standard. In the same way, usage trends come and go with regular circularity: we may condemn Tony Blair's use of **disinterested** to mean **uninterested** in his sound-bite description of a 'not disinterested, but disempowered' electorate, but this was, in fact, the very first meaning of the word when it evolved in the seventeenth century.

The point at which an incorrect use becomes acceptable is one of the hardest things for a lexicographer to determine. Modern dictionary-makers, to the chagrin of many, describe language more than they prescribe it: they reflect changes of meaning without the subjective commentary of earlier recorders such as Samuel Johnson or, later, the Fowler brothers. A lack of overt condemnation does not, however, make today's dictionaries unmediated free-for-alls documenting every shift in our vocabulary. Current dictionaries also give a strong indication of where something is regarded as wrong. Linguistic change—spellings such as **miniscule** (rather than **minuscule**), for example, or the decline of **fewer**—are often given extended treatment which offers clear guidance, even as it charts current trends.

Correct usage is a fierce battleground which has much to do with social and cultural norms, including class and education. A key criterion in judging correctness is clarity; confusion in language robs it of the capacity for discriminated expression. A degree of linguistic discipline is therefore essential. When that discipline is lost—as, for example, in jargon or in lazy pronunciation—the result can be obfuscation and frustration. At the same time it is important to recognize that the boundaries of that discipline are elastic, allowing for creativity of expression and even a deliberate flouting of rules for a particular effect. Good writing stretches language as well as the imagination.

The following documents some of the changing trends in English usage. Whether or not they threaten to supersede the existing order is debatable; what is certain is that the linguistic status quo will not be a permanent one.

The personal treatment

There is an increasing tendency in official literature to adapt an individual's voice through the use of the first person singular. The effort is made in part to avoid the formal-sounding passive voice, and to achieve simplicity (particularly for non-native speakers of English), but is also part of a general move towards intimacy. Today's British tax forms, for example, will state that 'I have sent you two forms', or that 'I have calculated from the information you provided that you owe...', etc. Such examples go against traditional teaching which dictates that the first person should never be used in documents which intend to inform: 'I' is to be used to express sentiment only.

Today, authority seems to go hand in hand with an appeal to personal experience, a connection clearly made by politicians as well as officials, whose aim is to achieve an ersatz intimacy for a specific purpose, be it wooing the electorate or softening bureaucracy. This casual approach was evident in many of the slogans produced during the 2005 British election, including the Conservative Party's 'I mean, how hard is it to keep a hospital clean?'. Noticeable too is the use of the continuous present which, as well as sounding dynamic, is intended to reassure, as in a local council's stated aim of 'Caring for the Community' or the British Council's promise of 'Creating Opportunities Worldwide'.

Shifting senses: fortunate or fortuitous?

It is perfectly normal for single words to have several meanings, and for their meanings to change over time. It is also quite common for a word or phrase to acquire a meaning for which another word or phrase already exists. Those who are sensitive to such changes often deplore them, particularly if the language seems to shrink or become more diffuse as a result, and most particularly if the shift is occurring because one word is being confused with another.

Fifty years ago, commentators objected to many substitutions that are now unremarkable, as for example in the use of **claim** for **assert**; of **disincentive** for **deterrent**; of **feel** for **think**; of **sadism** for **cruelty**; and of **hairdo** for **coiffeur** (the former loathed for its casualness). Below is a list of words and phrases that may also be in the process of acquiring new meanings. Some are so well established in their new roles that they already appear in this guise in modern dictionaries, though often with a brief note explaining their parvenu status.

- **mitigate** for **militate**: 'Would it not be a good idea if British and US companies with the technology to establish energy plants in those countries could do so, to mitigate against the effects of fossil fuel pollution?' This question, posed by Conservative MP Nigel Evans during a parliamentary debate, confuses two unrelated terms. To 'mitigate' is to make something less severe or serious; to 'militate', almost always used with 'against', is to be a powerful factor in preventing something. Oxford's language databases suggest that 10% of current uses are incorrect.

- **on behalf of** for **on the part of**, or **by**: the British parliamentary record Hansard quotes Lord McIntosh of Haringey as saying: 'The whole point of the Financial Services Authority is to stop people's careers, businesses and finances being destroyed by bad behaviour on behalf of those in the financial community.'

- **reticent** for **reluctant**: an Irish seismologist, credited with having foretold the March 29 Indian Ocean earthquake, was reported to have commented: 'We are very reticent to use the word "predict".' Examples of the confusion are in plentiful supply on the Internet.

- **fortuitously** for **fortunately**: 'fortuitous' means accidental, without the added idea of good luck that 'fortunately' brings. The two are starting to be used interchangeably.

- **momentarily** for **in a moment**: 'momentarily', in British English, means 'for a short time'. In US English it has the sense of 'very soon', a meaning which looks likely to establish itself in the UK too. For the time being, phrases such as the one used by airline staff 'we will be landing momentarily' can still cause consternation.

The politics of emotion

When Tony Blair spoke of seeking **closure** to the events leading to the death of arms expert David Kelly in 2003, he followed a trend in which the language of therapy and counselling is appropriated in markedly different contexts. Such emotive vocabulary, some of which dates back to the death of Diana, Princess of Wales, is frequently drawn on in political discourse. In the run-up to the 2005 British election, talk was of boosting the electorate's **self-esteem** to counteract their feeling of **disempowerment**.

The Iraq conflict found both George W. Bush and the British Prime Minister deliberately harnessing the emotive power of certain phrases. Tony Blair spoke of the **surging of the human spirit**; to the American people he declared: **We stand side by side with you now. Your loss we count as our loss. Your struggle we take as our struggle**. Rather than deploy the formal rhetoric of combat, each spoke on occasion of how they felt. As an adjunct, how the electorate 'feel' is now taken as an indicator directing national policy. As Munira Murza put it, writing in the online publication *Spiked*: 'Blair might run the country, but he presents himself as a man informally connected to us by emotion.' The Prime Minister has spoken frequently of **doing the right thing**, and of the fact that **I'm listening** (part in fact of the **Big Conversation**). As a result, Labour's **New Emotionalism** appeared in 2005 to direct its language as much as its political priorities.

The future of the present

A growing trend in news reports is what has been humorously dubbed predictive tensing, in which the public are told of statements and events that will happen, as opposed to those that have happened. Government papers and announcements are pre-empted by the news that the **Prime Minister will say at lunchtime**, or that the **White Paper will state...**, in which the actual is replaced by the 'scheduled-in-advance'.

Many saw the entire rationale of the British and US governments for the war on Iraq as being couched in terms of a possible future—of destruction—rather than an actuality. Commenting on the trend in the media, the *Guardian* columnist and comedy writer Armando Iannucci concluded: 'So we end up with the exact opposite of unreported facts, which is unfacted reports.'

Stringing along

The tendency to string compound adjectives together is a notable pattern in current discourse, and much contemporary jargon relies on it. The Higher Education Policy Institute called modern universities **client-focused, customer-centric**, and **outward-facing** all in one take, while the tendency to pile up attributive adjectives, often without hyphens, is also striking. One example from the Internet speaks of a **low cost easy to use web based document management system**.

Changing the past

Some forms of the past tense which have hitherto been unique to the US are beginning to appear in British English. **I snuck in round the back** and he dove into the pool without asking are now relatively commonplace in British English (**nosedived**, meanwhile, persists in the US, although there is evidence of **nosedove** creeping in). Similarly, the misuse of the past participle is on the increase: so we hear **I was stood at the bar** rather than the correct **I was standing at the bar**, or—to use an example from *Heat* magazine—**I was sat at home with my fat girlfriend having a Chinese**.

Sloppy speech?

A number of further trends in speech are emerging. The use of the double 'is' is becoming increasingly frequent: **the thing about it is, is that**. The false splitting of words is also evident: **a whole nother world** being one example. Meanwhile the fairly old habit of replacing 'with' with 'of' is gaining further currency: people are **fed up of** tabloid sensationalism. 'Of' also frequently occurs instead of 'have': '**I would of loved** to give the PM a piece of my mind.' This last example is more contentious; its use, for now at least, tends to be restricted to speech rather than written prose.

Extra fillings

'Fillers' such as **y'know** (a favourite of David Beckham and other foot-ballers as well as the British PM), **innit** (now an all-purpose filler used at the end of a statement and without a question mark), and **like**, and intensifiers such as **totally** and **literally**, continue to proliferate in current speech. Such is their frequency, particularly in slang, that they are beginning to function rather like 'er', 'um', and 'uh': fillers which we may take to be verbal white noise but which, some psycholinguists claim, fulfil an important role in helping the listener to process what they are hearing. 'Literally', for example, can deliver emphasis, comedy, and exaggeration depending on context.

Jargon

Every year thousands of examples of jargon come to the attention of the Plain Language Commission. Many are from official (including government) documentation in which clarity, it seems, falls victim to the inflationary principle: the belief that the more words used—and the more complex the better—the more important the writer will sound.

Jargon falls into a number of categories. It can operate as euphemism or spin (as in workplace jargon such as **downsizing** for the act of making someone redundant) or as a means of sounding important or cutting-edge. It can also be deliberately evasive.

In 2004 the Speaker of the House of Commons, Michael Martin, read out a judgement by the House of Lords on the then proposed Hunting Bill:

'The Lords insist on their amendments to the Hunting Bill to which the Commons have insisted on their disagreement, for which insistence they assign their reasons. They insist on their amendments to which the Commons have disagreed, for which insistence they assign their reasons, and they disagree to the amendment, proposed by the Commons in lieu of the Lords' amendments, for which disagreement they assign their reasons.'

Having read the statement out, Martin remarked: 'I read these messages. I don't understand them. It wasnae a Glasgow man who wrote that one anyway.'

Meanwhile an investment company reminded its customers: 'Please ensure that all registered holders complete and sign the enclosed Form of Renunciation. Due to a temporary issue we are currently unable to pre-populate all holders' names and addresses.'

The US Army Soldier Systems Center provided another example of the triumph of jargon over sense: 'The Combat Feeding Directorate actively leverages leading edge technologies to ensure the warfighter is provided the decisive edge in all aspects of combat feeding.'

A cucumber specification chart, given by a leading supermarket chain to its suppliers, also prompted some curious use of jargon. Women like cucumbers more than men, it seems (and so their tastes determine the ideal cucumber shape): a market analyst concluded somewhat obscurely that 'males of all ages under-index compared with total vegetables'.

Er-ring on the wrong side?

I went to the safe I'd built into my bedroom closet and took out the Smith &
Wesson. It's the one thing in the house I always keep clean: an automatic that
jams causes a lot more grief to the shooter than the shootee.
From *Guardian Angel*, by Sarah Paretsky, 1982.

There is currently an escalating fashion for constructing words with an
-ee suffix. The relationship between an agent **-er** and the direct or
indirect recipient of the action of that agent **-ee** (or 'doer' and 'doee') has a
reasonably long history. The concept of an **examiner** (1561), for example,
generates the corresponding idea of an **examinee** (1788), though most
'-er' and '-ee' pairings that are still in use did not arise until after 1800.
Apparently anomalous early examples, such as **pensioner** and **refugee**,
are most often accounted for by their having French roots.

The emergence (and sometimes brief life) of specific uses of the '-ee' suffix
can give an interesting sidelight on social history. **Dilutee** (1918) was a
term for an unskilled worker substituted, often controversially, for a skilled
one; while a **detainee**, defined by the *Oxford English Dictionary* as 'a
person detained in custody, usually on political grounds and in an
emergency, without or pending a formal trial', is first recorded in 1928.
In 1940s America, meanwhile, a **readjustee** was a person deemed to have
readjusted to civilian life. Today, this word is sometimes used to describe
someone who has undergone gender reassignment surgery.

'Readjustee' in its 1940s sense should logically be 'readjuster'. This switch
is fairly typical of American usage, where '-ee' is strongly understood to
enshrine a sense of weakness relative to another person or institution and
so on. Hence **escapee** (1875) means, not an ineffective prison guard, but an
escaped prisoner (an escaper, in fact); and an **attendee** (1961) is someone
who ('merely', in the words of the *OED*) attends something. These reversals
can lead to counter-instinctive or confusing usages. The opaque term
consentee refers to someone who has signed a consent form.

Subtle recalibrations of weakness achieved by adding the '-ee' suffix have given rise to an explosion of new terms, particularly but not exclusively in the US. A road accident victim is a **smashee** or **crashee**, while **strokee** now indicates someone who has suffered a stroke. Meanwhile the increasingly militant culture of fat appreciation in the US has led to the pairing of **feeder** and **feedee** (rather than 'eater'), to emphasize an unequal, sexualized relationship. In most cases the suffixes are used correctly; they are used because they are efficient.

Language in the Buff: The New Slang

14

Of the several ways in which slang sets out its stall as a subset of the English language, one of the most notable is its sheer inventiveness. The slang waterfront may be narrow—it is a world that deals in the easily accessible and concrete rather than the abstruse and abstract—but it is infinitely deep. The standard English word *drunk* is first recorded in 1340; it has served its purpose ever since. No formal collection of fourteenth-century slang exists but, by 1600, when slang glossaries had started appearing, a person could already be *boozy, in a merry pin, foggy, disguised, flyblown, in their cups, soused* and, if feeling sick, *casting up their accounts* for that single word 'drunk'. The modern English-speaking world offers a selection of around 3,000 synonyms.

Today, with a proliferation of hi-tech media spreading new words almost as fast as they appear, it is perhaps harder to acknowledge another identifying aspect of slang: that it is meant, at least at the time it is coined, to be secret. The user of slang, whether an all-out criminal or simply a teenager, deploys slang to provide a boundary, making those who know the vocabulary 'us' and those outside 'them'. The fact that outsiders inevitably scale the wall generates the need for constant invention. The areas that slang covers are perhaps limited, but the synonyms it coins are infinite.

Slang statistics

A study by one of today's leading chroniclers of slang, Jonathon Green, of half a millennium's worth of collected material—amounting to almost 100,000 words and phrases—shows the extent to which the same themes recur. Back in 1938, one J.Y.P.

Greig opined in the *Edinburgh Review* that 'the chief stimuli of slang are sex, money and intoxicating liquor'. Factoring in the relative new development of illicit drug-taking, together with the less openly celebrated bodily functions and a few choice insults, one has to conclude that Mr Greig had it right. A rough breakdown of the slang lexicon offers some illuminating statistics. Rounding off the figures, we find that, of those hundred thousand terms:

5,700 refer to crime and criminals

4,700 to drugs

4,600 to drink, drinking and drunkards

3,350 to money

2,500 to prostitutes and their pimps

2,400 to fools and foolishness

1,700 to the act of sexual intercourse

1,350 to the penis

1,300 to homosexuals and the gay world

1,200 to the vagina

1,000 to the policeman

960 to masturbation and masturbators

830 to dying or death

780 to madness

730 to beating and hitting

570 to racial stereotypes

560 to the anus and buttocks

470 to defecating and urinating

405 to murder

280 to ugliness

250 to fatness

220 to vomiting

Within these topics are further recurring themes. Sexual intercourse includes multiple variations on the idea of violence and of a man striking a woman (and occasionally getting struck in return): the term *fuck*, for example, may share a common origin with the Latin *pugno*, I fight, and *bang* is a further example of the link. Many of the synonyms for the state of being drunk or intoxicated suggest that the user/sufferer has been as often knocked to the ground as rendered 'high'.

What of contemporary slang? In terms of origin, Black American English has been conspicuously and consistently influential since the Second World War. This was not, of course, always the rule. Prior to that, in the UK at least, the primary source of slang was the criminal and non-criminal working class, with a substantial sidebar occupied by Cockney rhyming slang (a local dialect promoted to general slang through London's disproportionate influence in a small country). When, by the 1950s, the teenager—a product of US culture and rock 'n' roll, and typically American—appeared in the UK, slang took new instructions. For the teens of the 1950s, the beatniks, the hippies of the next decade, and for every variety of youth group ever since, Black America has been the primary source of twentieth and twenty-first-century slang. There is, however, one important difference: the speed with which the new slang is transmitted and then assimilated. With words like *cool* and *groovy*, the white beats and hippies, for instance, were drawing on American Black English and the lexicon of jazz, but the vocabulary took years, even decades, to cross the Atlantic. Today's coinages, even from the most inaccessible streets of New York or Los Angeles, are in the mouths of British youth within weeks. The Internet, the worldwide popularity of rap culture, movies, TV, and the international vocabulary of recreational drug use have all combined to spread and accelerate the take-up of slang.

The territory covered by the latest slang coinages includes sex, violence, verbal abuse, and drugs. This does not imply the disappearance of all that has gone before. Slang is by no means necessarily ephemeral, with some terms demonstrating remarkable longevity: *booze* for drink has been around since 1530, *birthday suit* for naked since the 1780s, and *pig* for policeman since 1800, and these are far from exceptional. Others, such as *joke*, *slum*, and *fake*, which all began as slang terms, have crossed over into standard English.

Sex is one area of slang in which many coinages are based on older usages: **on the chirps** is flirting; to fancy (itself a veteran term) or desire is to **feel** (one of today's all-purpose words, more generally used as 'empathize' or 'understand'), or to **love off**. The boy- or girlfriend is a **hubby** or **wifey** (terms that for once have definitely Anglo-Saxon origins) or a **boo** (from 'beau'); to two-time the partner is to **play** them. The promiscuous (from the male point of view) young woman is a **sket**, a **yat** or **yatty**, which can also mean a cowardly male, or a **Jezebel**, a term dating back to 1588 and relating to the biblical story of Jezebel. A woman who is **shyst** or **shysty** (thus the rapper Shystie) is sexually forward and generally aggressive. Her attractive sister is a **beanie** (also a 1950s hat worn off the face) and she is **tromp** or **trung** (both of which appear to be based on 'true'). To be sexually excited is to feel **jiggy** (which can double as simply nervous) while to **juice** or **juice up** is to stimulate and ultimately to have sex. To **kick it** or to be **on the link** (the physical linking together of the lovers—the eighteenth century offered *join giblets*) are also idioms meaning to have sexual intercourse, and intercourse itself is **the lash**: another example of sex as violence. To live with someone is to **crib**, a twenty-first-century use of a term that has been around since at least 1935, while 'crib' as a noun meaning a house, now back in vogue, is found in Shakespeare. To be **breeded up** is to be pregnant. The female breast is either a **rack** (an Americanism since the 1930s) or the **dairy** (already popular in 1780).

Sex appeal, or at least good (and bad) looks, is also rich terrain. Sex appeal itself is the echoic **boom-shi la**, reminiscent of the older *va-va-voom,* while **cris'**, a shortened form of 'crisp', means physically attractive (there is also an adverb, **crissly**), as does **fine** (and has done in Black America since the 1930s). Similar are **buff**, which stresses a physically toned body, **hot**, which has meant sexually attractive for more than a century, and **tick**. **Maaga**, from the French *maigre*, means thin and is a direct import from the West Indies. It can also be used of a 'meagre' state of mind. **Rank**, which started life meaning 'off' when referring to stale food, means unattractive or unpleasant, but **sick** (popular in surfing slang), in the long tradition of slang terms in which bad equals good, means excellent or 'cool'. In other cultures, **bindaas** means independent, attractive, and fashionable in Indian English, and **bowja** is a South African term for a good person. A **burqa babe** is a devout and attractive Muslim girl who manages to associate with the world beyond religion.

The body, plain or pretty, needs clothes, which can include **undercrackers** and **trollies**, both British synonyms for underpants. **Cris** and **buff** can refer to suits as well as their wearers, but something to be avoided is the **muffin top**: a 'spare tyre' of less than well-honed flesh, protruding between hipster trousers and a crop top. **Creps**, from a long-dead fashion for crêpe soles, are trainers, and **Tims** abbreviate Timberland boots. Finally a great survivor: **vine** has meant a suit since America's jazzmen coined it seventy years ago. Like the plant, it 'entwines' one's body.

Second only to clothes as a fashion statement are cars. The **whip** even sounds good, as opposed to the **hooptie**, the modern successor to the *junker* or *rattletrap*. Car of the moment in South Africa is the **G-string**, a BMW 3 series which presumably refers not to the world of lap dancing but to the **Gs** or urban **gangstas** whose ride of choice it is.

Wong (replacing *wonga*) still means money for the British (while Americans have **dead presidents**), as does **cheese**, which may have some jocular reference to *bread*, or possibly, at least when it was coined in the mid nineteenth century, to 'yellow' gold coins. More money terms include **ends**, as in **make ends meet**, and the long-lived standby **dough** (a veteran of the 1850s). **Spendy** means expensive while **braff** means worthless. One's business, whether as an occupation or simply a plan or situation, is **runnings**, another West Indian import. **Bait** refers to conspicuousness as in 'don't make it bait'.

On the less savoury side of the street lurks violence and its weaponry. To join a gang is to **go on line**. A gang fight is an **armshouse** (referring to the inevitable use of fire*arms*) or a **rockaz**, from 'ruckus', while a gun can be a **strap**, or a **bucky,** which is often homemade and 'bucks' in one's hand, or a **skeng**, which can also be a knife and may be linked to the West Indian **skengay**, a form of music in which the guitar sounds are seen as mimicking those of gunfire. One pulls the trigger and **busts a shot**. A **'chete** is a machete. To hit an opponent is to **rock** them **out**, to **bang** or **clap** them **up**. To steal, violently or otherwise, is to **tax** or **jack**, from the older *hijack*, and the thief, often working as a street mugger, is a **jacker**. To con someone out of their money is to **play** them **up** or **set** them **up**. The background to all this crime may be a rundown, sink estate, one that is **mashed up** or **down**. *Street*, the world of 'real life', which came on line twenty years ago, has been replaced by the synonymous **road**. A person's neighbourhood, once the *turf* or *manor*, is now an **end**.

◓

Drugs enjoy a vocabulary that goes beyond national or racial boundaries. **Chronic**, **hydro**, **sess**, **Buddha**, and **endo** / **indo** still mean super-strong cannabis in both the UK and US. To smoke cannabis is to **blaze** or **burn**. Drugs in general, whether **brown** (heroin) or **white** (crack cocaine), are **pharms**. Drug-dealing is **the Game** (an all-purpose descriptor, it has meant prostitution, gambling, and a variety of illegal activities). The dealer is a **shotter** who **busts shots** (sells drugs)—the links to gunfire are not coincidental. Dealer or user, drink or drug consumer, to **frontload** is what was once called *living* or *having it large*: enjoying the buzz of an extravagantly mind-manipulating lifestyle.

◓

Brer, as in brother (and of course Brer Rabbit), means a fellow black person. The biblical **bredrin** is synonymous (there is a **sistrin** too), while a **click** (i.e. clique) or **crew** is a gang of friends. A **jancrow** is a mean-spirited or bad man (or woman), adopted from Jamaican patois where John Crow is the carrion crow, while a **ginnygog** or **gog** is someone who is outstanding in some way. A **chief** is a fool, as is a **div** (in British English, where it is short for 'divvy'), a **neeky**, or **eedyot** (from 'idiot'). A **fascio** (perhaps from 'fascist') is another pejorative, often applied to the police or similar authorities; the **Feds**, borrowed from the US and filtered through TV and movies, are the police. **Fuckery**, which in the abstract means unfairness, ill-treatment, treachery, and nonsense, can refer to a person who personifies such characteristics and who may think themselves **all that**. A person who is annoying is **up in their hair** or **jarring**, and a coward is **shook**. A sycophant is a **kiss-arse**, **kiss-up**, **suck-up**, or **suck-butt**. **Ninja**, as in the black-clad super-fighters, means secretive. A **screwface** is the scowl affected by young men touting their macho 'attitude' and **stoush**—which may be linked to the same word in Australian English meaning a fight or brawl—means aggressive, hostile, and ready to fight.

◓

Slang takes no prisoners, but it is not universally negative. **Boom!**, and its clipped form **boo!**, means the very best; **grimey**, **heavy**, or **bashy** likewise. **Ova** (for 'over') cranks up a given adjective, thus **ova-grimey** means really, really good, **ova-buff** exceptionally cute. **Reallion** sounds meaningless but probably comes from the idea of 'real' as in *keeping it real*, and again means good, as in 'that's straight-up reallion'. Equally popular is **braaap!**, echoic like the earlier American **booyaka!** of the thump of a gunshot; again, it is used to praise. **Bare**, meaning lots of, is another one for multi-tasking: *bare dough* means lots of cash, *bare jokes* very funny, and so on.

For some, slang is the ultimate sign of language going downhill. The rich and vibrant examples available to us today, covering the same areas which have attracted it throughout history, argue the opposite. Slang is one of the most liberated showcases language can offer, suggesting robustness and vitality; growth not decline.

Hound Dog Day: The Political Animal

15

Hyenas feast on bill—but they're not laughing.
> Simon Hoggart in *The Guardian*, March 2005, describing the debate in the House of
> Lords over Labour's controversial Prevention of Terrorism Bill. 'It was like watching a pack
> of hyenas fall upon the rotting corpse of a wildebeest.' Another of Hoggart's columns was
> headlined **Bones of contention over a dog's breakfast**.

**The Express, which used to love Blair and eat biscuits at his tea table, has turned
into an attack dog biscuit. It will carry on a hyena howl of hate far beyond next
spring.**
> Peter Preston in *The Observer*, October 2004.

**Old yellow dogs can learn new tricks, too—the official weblog of the Democratic
Party is called the Yellow Dog Blog.**
> Texas Politics website, 2005.

In March 2005, an interview between a notoriously incisive and
confrontational television presenter and the British Health Secretary
prompted an extraordinary on-screen argument which resounded in the
media for days afterwards, and which looks set to have made a lasting
impact on political idiom.

The subject of debate in the interview of John Reid by Jeremy Paxman on
the BBC's daily political analysis programme *Newsnight*, was Labour's
health plans, a key battleground in the run-up to Britain's general election.
Paxman described Reid as an **attack dog** for his party, and in doing so
drew on a well-worn political metaphor, one much used in the US
presidential contest when the Democrats' vice-presidential candidate John

Edwards attracted the same epithet. Reid's response was immediate, and hostile: 'If you have a PhD and a posh accent from a school like yours,' he told Paxman, 'you are regarded as a sophisticate... You called me an attack dog because I've got a Glasgow accent.'

The key difference between the use of the phrase in the presidential election and that by Paxman lies in the respective responses to it. Fox TV, which was among the first to use it in reference to John Edwards, was subsequently accused of political bias. John Reid, on the other hand, perceived it as a direct accusation of class prejudice. The *Newsnight* spat was not the only such incident in the heated political climate of early 2005, when allegations of bias were rife. Not all were 'calling the class card' (as one *Times* journalist saw it); others involved alleged racial and religious slurs. The British Leader of the Opposition, Michael Howard, saw himself as a frequent target; in a speech to his party's pre-election spring forum he alluded to—later discarded—political advertisements for the Labour Party: 'So far this year they have compared me to Fagin, to Shylock and to a flying pig. I don't know about you, but something tells me that someone, somewhere out there, is just a little bit rattled.'

It was Howard who became the subject of more 'attack dog' imagery. A fresh war of words began after he was dubbed an **attack mongrel** by the former Labour Leader of the Commons Peter Hain. Tory officials seized on the term as further evidence of anti-Semitism against the Jewish Howard. Ironically, it was a Tory politician who had previously run into trouble over the use of the word 'mongrel': John Townend, a Conservative backbencher, caused uproar in 2001 after he warned of Britain becoming a **mongrel race** through immigration. In 2005, some sections of the British media launched a campaign to curb Gypsy encampments, a cause picked up by the Conservative Party who were described as campaigning on **dog-whistle politics**: populist themes targeted at very specific sections of the electorate (see pages 55–56).

The image of the political dog, be it of the aggressive or cross-breed variety, is far from new. Its usefulness was evident almost a century ago when the Liberal government's budget of 1909 sparked the twentieth century's first constitutional crisis—the Lords rejected proposals to introduce radical measures to redistribute tax and finance social provisions such as the old age pension. In the course of the debate, David Lloyd George said dismissively of the House of Lords and Arthur Balfour respectively: 'The lean and trusty **mastiff** which is to watch over our interests, but which runs away at the first snarl of the trade unions. . . . A mastiff? It is the right hon. Gentleman's **poodle**. It fetches and carries for him. It barks for him. It bites anybody that he sets it on to.' The direct confrontation resulted in the Parliament Act of 1911, which removed the Lords' veto.

The poodle image has proved a resilient one: in 2004 and 2005 Tony Blair was frequently described as the lapdog of the same breed to George W. Bush and his causes. In the aftermath of the 'attack dog' incident a *Times* cartoon presented a new take on the 2005 Crufts dog show: above the caption 'Best in Show', one dog—labelled 'attack mongrel' and clearly portraying Michael Howard—sinks its teeth into the poodle image of Tony Blair.

In the political world the dog can, it seems, carry with it an infinite set of associations, according to the context and to the speaker's will. Shakespeare's Coriolanus spoke to the people of Rome as 'you common cry of **curs**', while the 'attack dog' metaphor has echoes of the words Shakespeare gives Mark Antony in *Julius Caesar*: **Cry 'Havoc!' and let slip the dogs of war**. Clement Attlee, speaking of his Foreign Secretary, pronounced in 1960 his belief that **It's a good maxim that if you have a good dog you don't bark yourself. I had a very good dog in Mr Ernest Bevin**. The English historian and political philosopher Arnold Toynbee likened America in the 1970s to **a large, friendly dog in a very small room. Every time it wags its tail it knocks over a chair**, while, in Australia, Bill Hayden, bumped from the Labor leadership, infamously commented in 1983 that **a drover's dog could lead the Labor Party to leadership the way the country is**, thus propelling 'like a drover's dog' into popular Australian usage. More forgivingly perhaps, Bill Clinton's wife Hillary described her husband, after his admissions during 'Monicagate', as **a hard dog to keep on the porch**.

In the US, the term **yellow dog Democrat** continues to hold currency. The term 'yellow dog' derives from a saying which emerged during the 1928

presidential election: 'I'd vote for a yellow dog if he ran on the Democratic ticket.' In that year's presidential election campaign, the yellow dog Democrats were Alabamans who remained loyal to the party in spite of their dissatisfaction with the Democratic candidate, Al Smith. The expression retains its associations of the Southern Democrats' extreme loyalty.

After the Republicans won the majority in the US House of Representatives in 1994, a group of thirty-three conservative Democrats formed the **Blue Dog Coalition**, blue being the colour of Democratic wins on the election map. The Blue Dogs represent a stronger break from the national and more liberal Democratic Party, and date back to the 1980s when a group of Democrats crossed party lines to support some of Ronald Reagan's policies.

Linguistic alliances with politics often show greater longevity than those in power. The imagery of the dog, thanks to its vast possibilities of breeds and dispositions, is persistent, and seems perfectly suited to political endeavour. As one term becomes a rare breed, a new canine moniker appears. Just as the metaphor of lions led by asses is resurrected during warfare, so poodles and attack dogs are unleashed at times of major political battles—or dogfights.

Catchphrases through the Looking Glass

16

The term 'catchphrase' originated in the middle of the nineteenth century, when it denoted a phrase which was sufficiently interesting or plausible to appeal to the unsophisticated and uneducated: to catch their attention. If today the social or opportunistic implications of the term have been lost, the requisite of interest remains. For some catchphrases, that interest can be sustained for decades.

There is a fascinating cultural history to be written about the catchphrases which gained currency over a century ago, many of which did so through the theatre and music hall. A comparison of catchphrases in the past with those today is as expressive of social and attitude change as is the evolution of our vocabulary.

To illustrate this, we might follow the history of an individual catchphrase. **Chase me, Charley** is recorded in dictionaries of historical slang as a kind of saucy synecdoche of the nineteenth century's 'Naughty Nineties' and Edwardian era. It seems to arise from a music hall song of that name with, according to a theatre review in *The Era* (2 September 1899), 'the lady who is responsible for this somewhat enigmatic expression being a lady of uncertain age, but certain intentions in the matrimonial line'. It consisted of typical music hall lyrics (here with the spelling 'Charlie') sung to the tune of the 'Gay Gordons' ('Cock of the North'):

Chase me Charlie, Chase me Charlie, Lost the leg of my drawers
Chase me Charlie, Chase me Charlie, Please will you lend me yours?

The title, which has endured as an example of cockney songs (or 'ding dongs') alongside 'It's a Long Way to Tipperary' and 'Knees Up Mother Brown', was used as the name of a 1917–18 compilation of Charlie Chaplin short films. Both song and film are also alluded to in James Joyce's *Ulysses* and *Finnegans Wake*, and the song in Sean O' Casey's *Windfalls*. It is also the name of a completely different song from the Noel Coward musical *Ace of Clubs*.

Chase me, Charley is recorded as a catchphrase in the *Oxford English Dictionary* from 1906. In the Second World War it was used as the name of a German guided bomb. It is mentioned in Peter and Iona Opie's *Children's Games in Street and Playground* in 1969 as the name of a children's chasing game played in water. It also appears to have been used as a slogan by supporters of Charles Haughey in the Irish elections of the 1980s. Even more recently, 'Chase me Charlie, Chase me Charlie, Pull the string of my drawers' is recalled as a playground chant in a Google newsgroup (1998), and it is common in equestrian circles as the name for a gymkhana equivalent of the *puissance*.

That a hundred-year-old catchphrase is still finding resonance today is quite remarkable; it has done so by shifting its point of reference. There are other phrases in use today which may well demonstrate the same versatility.

In the 1992 US election, Bill Clinton's political strategist James Carville placed a sign over his desk in the Little Rock headquarters of the campaign, which read **It's the economy, Stupid!** For a campaigner fixed on a need for a central theme, the sign was a pithy response to the question of what Clinton's campaign was all about.

Carville's words remain a formulaic reminder of a central issue or goal in any political situation. In 2005 Tony Blair set out to woo environmentalists by plugging into a growing body of academic work that seeks to develop alternatives to gross domestic product as a yardstick of the quality of life, such as good health, a safe environment, and strong communities. The move was seen as an attempt to remind the electorate that Labour strategy was not single-stranded: in other words **it's not only the economy, stupid**. The reconfiguration also held a tacit allusion to the Prime Minister's allegedly complicated and competitive relationship with his Chancellor Gordon Brown. Ironically, when Gordon Brown stepped firmly onto the pre-election campaign wagon, the headlines returned to the original, concluding that, for Blair in 2005, his Chancellor was a key bargaining chip with the British public.

There is good evidence that the catchphrase is branching out. Adaptations such as **it's the tax hike, stupid, it's the oil, stupid**, and **it's the race issue, stupid** are plentiful. On the letters page of *The Guardian* in April 2005, a professor at the University of Birmingham's School of Biosciences, Graham Martin, wrote simply: 'If a politician ever said that the principal issue of the day was "**our ecology, stupid**", he would be saying something true and wise.' Whatever the variation, the resonance of the phrase is constant: it identifies the one salient fact which is beyond debate, but which the audience seems to need reminding of.

A further topical example of such a formula is **the only gay in the village**, a much-repeated catchphrase from the British comedy series *Little Britain*. In their beginnings, tied to their original source, phrases such as these can bring a sense of unity among viewers: by drawing on the stock of catchphrases from a particular programme, an individual signals a belonging to a certain club. It is if and when a catchphrase takes off, however, that it becomes really interesting. Extensions of the *Little Britain* formula include the **only lesbian/bisexual/queer/Catholic in the village**, while the general election spawned a string of spin-offs, of the only **Tory/socialist/Liberal in the village** variety.

These are some of the many catchphrases which lodge themselves in the language. Those that last are the ones which can be reapplied easily to new contexts, or which have the versatility to allow individual elements to be varied.

Crunking and Shoegazing: New Musical Expression

17

The musical sound and word of 2005 was **crunk**: 'America's hottest urban music style, a rowdy, boys-together style of southern hip-hop', according to *The Guardian*. Less well known in Britain, in the US it is popular enough to have generated several new offshoot terms. The nineteen-year-old R & B singer Ciara has been hailed for her **crunk 'n' b**, while rock band *Korn* have experimented with **crunk rock**. **Crunk-lite**, meanwhile, is a form likely to be sneered at by dedicated (or **crunked-up**) **crunksters**.

The word 'crunk' is often held to be a mixture of 'crazy' and 'drunk', although the chief exponent of the style, Lil Jon, sees it differently: 'Crunk is a term used in the south as long as I can remember ... It means high energy. It don't have nothing to do with getting crazy drunk—you can get crunk without getting drunk at all ... In Atlanta, we live and die to get crunk' (*Echoes* magazine).

The nearest UK equivalent to crunk is **grime**, an offshoot of the **UK garage** scene that developed in London's East End. Characterized by rapid rapping over electronic bleeps and deep bass sounds, grime is also known as **sub-low** or **eski**.

Partly because it is such a catchy word, and partly because it appears to have arisen organically rather than as a coinage from a single source, 'crunk' is a term that both performers and journalists are happy to use. Other names for musical styles, however, can take a little longer to become established and accepted, as has been the case with **shoegazing** and **Krautrock**, both of which have recently been added to the *Oxford English Dictionary*.

Shoegazing is a style of rock music that originated in southern England in the early 1990s, epitomized by groups such as *Ride* and *Slowdive*. These groups favoured a blurred, dreamy sound, and their performances were characterized by a rather reticent style in which the members tended to look down, especially to operate the effects pedals that produced their 'cathedrals of sound' (a favourite term of description), rather than at the audience. 'Shoegazing' was first recorded in 1991, in the *New Musical Express* (*NME*), but has become more widely used since the turn of the century, with a revival of interest in the genre. The music was at first known as **dreampop** in the US, but this seems to have fallen from favour, and American fans are now gazing footwear-wards too.

Krautrock dates back further, to 1972 (it also first appeared in the *NME*). Although 'Kraut', for 'German', is a derogatory term dating back to the First World War, 'Krautrock' is not intended as an insult; it refers to an experimental style of German rock with a robotic, futuristic, synthetic sound. Again, the term has been largely confined to aficionados through most of its history but it has recently assumed a higher profile, with the continuing influence of Krautrock bands such as *Can* and *Kraftwerk*.

The history of the music press is littered with terms for minor genres that were coined and energetically used by a particular writer or publication but never really became established. Who remembers **fraggle** or **romo** today? Since the 1990s, music and the music press have been increasingly polarized into a multitude of different styles and attendant publications. In the 1970s, rock was covered in Britain largely by the *New Musical Express*, *Melody Maker*, and *Sounds*, with black musical forms such as soul and disco receiving little serious coverage. Today there are racks of publications covering what used to be called 'heavy metal', but can now be **black metal**, **death metal**, **hair metal**, **nu-metal**, **speed metal**, **thrash metal**, or just plain **metal**; rock, meanwhile, can be **art rock**, **avant-rock**, **blues rock**, **folk rock**, **funk rock**, **glam rock**, **jazz rock**, **math rock**, **noise rock**, **poodle rock**, **pop rock**, **prog rock** (i.e. 'progressive'), **sludge rock**, **space rock**, **surf rock**—even **post-rock**, a term that in theory should mark the end of the whole parade of styles, but which in reality is likely to be just one of the long list of brave new forms.

Dance music is split into even more categories than rock. Some genre names were apparently coined as a joke but have stuck, for example **handbag**, a form of house music characterized by its catchy melodies and upbeat mood. It took its name from the image of women who dance in a circle with their handbags at their feet, intending to be suggestive of the music's unsophisticated, crowd-pleasing quality. So established has it become that it has given rise to a more techno-influenced offshoot, **hardbag**.

The development of a private, in-crowd language that excludes the unhip is another attribute of musical terminology. The multiplicity of genres, often created by combining terms to create ever more subdivisions (**neo-pop**, **acid-trance**, **indie-dance**), is part of this. Another is the coining of new words by adding characteristic prefixes and suffixes. The suffix **-core** comes from **hardcore**, a name for various types of extreme or aggressive music, but can now be tagged on to any noun or adjective to create an instant genre name. Recent examples include **sad-core** (presumably a determinedly depressing style), **jah-core** (a band combining reggae and punk), **fox-core** (played by 'foxy chicks'), **cuddle-core** (a female group from Canada), **nerd-core**, and **prog-core**.

The saying goes that 'writing about music is like dancing about architecture'. However true, the determination to pin down new genres— and the consequent rate of name-coining—seems unlikely to abate.

Smoothing Out the Wrinkles: **18**
The Language of Cosmetics

In the factory we make cosmetics; in the store we sell hope.
Charles Revlon of Revlon Cosmetics, 1960s.

Cosmetic results

The word **cosmetic** has a dubious feel. **Cosmetics** are beauty products: Tobias Smollett refers in 1755 to 'cosmetic slops and washes'. **Cosmetic surgery**, a term which came into use in the aftermath of the First World War, refers to invasive and sometimes drastic procedures to improve the appearance. Nevertheless, 'cosmetic' also means superficial, and an air of frivolousness and impermanence attaches to it in all its uses. This may be why **reconstructive surgery** is now a preferred usage for procedures performed on, for example, the victims of car accidents, and why one upmarket cosmetics company now markets its foundation as 'perfectly real make-up'.

Looking good: feeling better

The benefits of looking good are hard to measure. They can, however, stretch to feeling good, which is supposed, in turn, to make you look even better. The cosmetics industry promotes this more or less conscious **placebo** effect in its customers, even though the results are only temporary. Only in the early nineteenth century was 'placebo' defined as 'any medicine adapted more to please than benefit the patient'. For at least five centuries beforehand it had carried the meaning of a flatterer, sycophant, or parasite. These days it is unremarkable that a moisturizer will offer the user *Total Comfort*, that a face wash 'wakes you up', and that a shower gel is marketed as *Anti Stress Therapy*. A typical eyelid cream can be billed as *Intelligent Balance Night Fluid Uplifting Eye Cream*, intelligence, balance, and uplift being qualities one might more sensibly hope to deploy in dealings with the mind or soul rather than with the skin.

Therapy

The health and beauty industries are adept both at redefining problems and at dressing up their cures, as the explosion of therapies now available shows. Among those on offer are **hippotherapy**: the use of horse riding to treat psychological and physical problems (from the Greek *hippos* meaning horse); **mesotherapy**: in which injections are given to break down fatty deposits under the skin (from *mesoderm*, the parts of the body such as bone, fat, and the muscles derived from the middle layer of cells or tissues of an embryo, from Greek *mesos* 'middle' and *derma* 'skin'); **algotherapy**: involving being wrapped in a warm seaweed paste; **fangotherapy**: being covered in mud, which has supposedly health-giving properties (from the Italian *fango*, meaning mud); **vinotherapy**: being massaged or covered with the flesh, skin, and seed of grapes to benefit from their antioxidant properties; **phytotherapy**: the use of plants and plant-derived products for massage, and also used to refer to herbal medicine (from Greek *phuton* 'a plant'); and **chocotherapy**: the application of cocoa and cocoa butter on the outside of the body to promote positive chemical and detoxifying reactions.

The poisonous arts

The term **detox** became current in the 1970s, and referred then to drug withdrawal systems and the clinics where they were implemented ('I'm going into detox'). 'Detox' has since been appropriated by the health and beauty industry for more general use, and can be loosely applied to diets, face creams, hair products, and so on. The assumed appeal of purity in this context is in marked contrast to the success of the poison **Botox** (botulinum toxin), which temporarily paralyses muscle, and is used to stun wrinkles. Botox has become increasingly popular and is in common parlance as both a noun and a verb (as in 'You can tell she's been botoxed').

Plump and dimpled

The words **plump** and **dimpled** have also moved on in the world of beauty. Dimples used to be found in the cheeks of happy women, and the cheeks and chins of men, and were extolled for their great loveliness. Shakespeare, in *Antony and Cleopatra*, wrote of 'Pretty dimpled boys, like smiling Cupids'. Now, however, 'dimpled' is ruthlessly associated with unnecessary **cellulite** (a non-technical term for subcutaneous fat) on women's hips and upper legs, an affliction known also as **orange-peel thighs**. For the first time in history, dimpled cheeks can be thought of as a disaster. Plumpness, by contrast, has for some decades been tutted over by a beauty industry that vaunts being thin. Nevertheless, 'plump' has recently been rehabilitated as the word of choice to describe beautiful lips. More or less invasive **lip plumpers**, which offer a look of full, **bee-stung** lips (a term dating back to 1858), are so much the rage that their excessive use has spawned the derisive term, the **trout pout**.

Colour blind?

Many cosmetic, underwear, and hosiery companies continue to use such labels as **nude**, **flesh**, **barely there**, and **naked** for off-white products aimed at women with pale skin (all of which carry the kind of sexual undertones frequently found in the vocabulary of fashion and cosmetics). Two other terms in this bracket are **neutral** and **natural**, the latter a serious misnomer given the prejudice inherent in implying that darker skin hues are unnatural. Some companies do take steps to avoid this area of offence, using instead **champagne**, **porcelain**, **ivory**, **cameo**, and so on. The ubiquity of coffee shops, and the glamorously foreign words they have popularized, also allows for instant grasp of designations along the lines of **cappuccino** or **hint of mocha**. Awkwardness about the naming of skin-related products would seem to explain the bet-hedging of a popular lipstick called **Natural Latte**.

Paranoid Gunk

Lipstick colour names, an imprecise but suggestive area of language use, are changed regularly, and thus give a good sense of what is deemed by the industry to be fashionable. No doubt shades offered under the title **Dusky Rose** will always have their customers, but the mainstream market now has a raw and highly sexualized front end, where the names only glancingly suggest a colour at all. **Lust**, **Nude Juice**, **Snog**, and **Screamer** are all readily available on the high street. One cosmetic company that has taken this trend to an extreme is Urban Decay, which feels compelled to provide explanations for those of its product terms that are hard to interpret. For a start it sells not lipstick but **Lip Gunk**, described as 'stuff for your lips'. **Gunk** was actually patented as a proprietary product in 1932, being a 'self-emulsifying colloidal detergent solvent', but the word was rapidly absorbed into English, where it now rubs shoulders with **goo**. Urban Decay's posture of rebellion leads to product colour names such as **Stray Dog**, **Gash**, **Asphyxia**, and **Bitten**. Once again, translations are in order, with the perhaps disappointing revelation that the Lip Gunk colour **Paranoid** is glossed as **Honeycomb**.

Feel visibly different

The word **visible** has been adopted industry-wide as the guarantee of a worthwhile face cream ('wrinkles appear visibly reduced'), while for other remedial products **effective** is the norm. Assertions that an antiperspirant is effective, or that the user of a face cream will see a visible difference, do raise the question of how big the market can be for ineffective antiperspirants, or for creams producing a result that you cannot see. Such logical oddities might be explained away as unconsidered by-products of inflationary language use (see *Bigging It Up*, pages 48–51). Unlike 'effective', however, the term 'visible', though couched as a guarantee, seems to hint at equivocation. Most face creams induce temporary plumpness in the skin. Temporarily, it will be true that wrinkles 'appear' visibly reduced, but the claim stops short of the more definitive 'wrinkles reduced'.

Poisons and potions a century ago

A hundred years ago, what were known in England as the **toilet arts** involved far more poisons than today's Botox regime. Simultaneously however, there was a detox vogue based on the idea that blood purification could improve absolutely everything. Many products were promoted on the promise that they would clean the blood: liver pills especially, but also digestive aids, one of the simplest home remedies being the consumption of paraffin.

Perceived health and beauty problems in 1905 were manifold, and included **hideous mouse marks** (a type of facial blemish), the desire for increase of chest measurement, the frankly described **offensive perspiration of the feet**, **extreme redness of the nose** (unattractive in itself, and liable to give the impression of the bearer being a drunkard), pinched looks due to **brain fag**, and the desperate need to achieve **hand whitening**, 'a task which every member of the fair sex is anxious to accomplish'.

Unlike today, there was a marked emphasis on concocting remedies at home. Though a few remain standard ingredients, much else on the 1905 shopping list is now incomprehensible, illegal, or both. **Dentifrice** (toothpaste or powder) could be made from **cuttlefish bone** and honey; standard depilatories (hair removers) were made with **quicklime**; while face creams, hair stains, nose douches, and the like were thrown together out of such components as **spermaceti** (the head fat of sperm whales), **otto of rose** (*otto* being a variant of attar or essence: *ottoed* was used to mean 'scented'), **sulphur** counted in **scruples** (twenty-grain measures), **lead**, **talk** (*talc*), **balsam of Peru** (*balsam* is a general term for an aromatic resin), **boric acid**, **mercury** derivatives (including **corrosive sublimate**), **potash**, **rectified spirit** (distilled alcohol), **oil of neroli** (a bitter orange essential oil, named after an Italian princess), **arsenic**, and **Carlsbad salt**. The danger of putting corrosives into hand and face creams was acknowledged in warnings to women that, before using these products, they should remove their jewellery, not only for fear that the metal would be eaten away, but to avoid gemstones falling out of their settings. The purpose of such creams was to whiten and smooth the skin (whiteness being seen as a sign of gentility, since only workers were exposed to the sun for any period).

Less dangerous techniques in 1905 for avoiding wrinkles included the suggestion that a woman retain her body fat, and assume a bland demeanour. Modern press hysteria surrounding **heroin chic** and anorexia find a bizarre echo in the writing of a hundred years ago, when beauty experts anxiously condemned the belief that consumption (tuberculosis) was desirable because it conferred on sufferers a 'transparent delicacy of the complexion'.

Make-up

Cosmetics in 1905 were primitive, and a genteel lady would admit to using only three types: white, pink, and black. White cosmetics made the face paler, an effect every woman was encouraged to seek, though Charles Dickens' magazine, *All the Year Round*, described the consequence at worst as a 'ghastly cosmeticised whiteness'. Pink cosmetic, or **rouge**, was used exclusively for heightening the cheeks; and black cosmetic, in paste form, was used only to emphasize the eyebrows. Any other products were in theory left to women of loose morals, and actresses. At this time, the concept of **making up** the face was still theatre slang. Cora Brown Potter, actress and previously a friend of the Prince of Wales, admitted in 1905 that one could use a black preparation, finely applied like a modern eyeliner, to 'throw up the eyes', but did not choose to reveal any other of the subtle and complex arts at her disposal.

Angelic

In 1905, discussions of beauty went hand in hand with extreme moralizing. The Bible says of Jezebel, shortly before she came by her deserts, that 'she tired [attired] her hair, and she painted her face'. No matter how much arsenic, mercury, or lead you applied, there could be no cure for a woman whose attractions were on the wane because she had been 'hardened and branded by the indelible stigma of sin'. Yet there was hope for all who aspired to be good, and who believed that we can 'illumine the little sphere we shine in, till we radiate an angel's light in a dark and sordid world'. In 2005, moralizing of this kind has disappeared from the mainstream, but the celestial language has found a new home all over the jars. Anyone with some spare cash can buy themselves immediate uplift: *Pure Energy Daily Radiance Cream...For Instant Illuminating Radiance.*

Crinolines and Chuddies: The Language of the Undergarment

19

> However you may tell her as a friend gradually to reduce her Stuffing as Rumps are quite out in France and are decreasing here but can not be quite given up 'till the weather grows warmer.
>
> E. Sheridan in his journal, 1786, quoted in the *Oxford English Dictionary*.

> Satan himself can't save a woman who wears thirty-shilling corsets under a thirty-guinea costume.
>
> 'In the Interests of the Brethren' from Rudyard Kipling's *Debits and Credits*, 1926.

> Pirate: I'm gonna teach you the meaning of pain.
> Elizabeth: You like pain? Try wearing a corset.
>
> From the film *Pirates of the Caribbean*, 2004.

> Memoirs of a basque revolutionary.
>
> Headline of a *Times* tribute to Janet Reger, who died in March 2005.

The death in 2005 of Janet Reger, the doyenne of luxurious underwear, prompted many retrospectives of a career which was seen to have single-handedly revolutionized the design of female underwear. Writing in *The Times*, Lisa Armstrong wrote: 'Whether Reger made sexy underwear respectable or respectable underwear sexy is a moot point: probably she did both.' From wearing liberty bodices and strictly functional white, beige, or plaster-of-Paris pink petticoats, knickers, and bras, women began to embrace basques and thongs. Such was Reger's success that her name became shorthand for the underwear she created. Tom Stoppard's 1978 play *Night and Day* included the line: 'Don't get your Janet Regers in a twist.'

In their style, Reger's knickers were in fact the antithesis of the much-discussed 'big pants' worn by the eponymous heroine in *Bridget Jones's Diary*, voted as the subject of the 'top movie moment' in a 2005 poll of cinemagoers. In the US version of the original book, those same pants are called **grannie pants**.

Later in the same month, the tour of singer and style icon Kylie Minogue made front-page news. Descriptions of her music were minimal; rather it was to Kylie's sixteen-inch waist that the tabloids devoted hundreds of column inches, thus announcing the latest stage in the evolution of the **corset**. Over its long lifetime the garment has been variously perceived as a symbol of female oppression, as a suit of armour protecting women's morality, and as a form of erotic bondage. Its incarnation today is portrayed as one of self-confident, strong female sexuality, evident in the new taste for the burlesque and for exotic and expensive lingerie. The corset has even been reclaimed by some feminists who see it as an empowerment of sexuality, akin to the male codpiece. Such shifts in the symbolism of women's fashion have long been reflected in its lexicon.

'Corset' itself is first recorded in the *Oxford English Dictionary* in 1299. It is a diminutive form of the Old French word *cors* meaning body, and is defined as 'a close-fitting body-garment; especially a laced bodice worn as an outside garment by women in the middle ages and still in many countries; also a similar garment formerly worn by men'. The later sense, which still holds currency, of a close-fitting inner bodice stiffened by whalebone and fastened by lacing to give shape and support to the figure, dates back to the late eighteenth century. *The Times* provides the *OED*'s first citation, from 1795, 'Corsettes about six inches long, and a slight buffon tucker of two inches high, are now the only defensive paraphernalia of our fashionable Belles.'

The term 'corset' survived in spite of Victorian prudery, which ensured that another staple of female underwear, the **bustle**, was referred to by the French words **tournure**, **pannier**, or **crinolette** in order to avoid vulgarity. By comparison, some modern terms, such as **peek-a-boo knickers** and **baby-dolls**, deliberately combine both coyness and sexiness.

The use of French words to provide linguistic soft focus was not new.
Pantalettes, describing long underpants with a frill at the bottom of each
leg, and worn by women and girls in the nineteenth century, **chemisettes**
(similar to today's **camisole**, another French borrowing), and **corselettes**
—all with the diminutive '-ette' suffix—made an entrance in the
nineteenth century. Another French word, **lingerie** (meaning 'linen')
earlier denoted the white garments in a woman's wardrobe, including cuffs
and handkerchiefs; it was not until the 1890s that it became synonymous
with underwear. **Linen** itself also denoted undergarments, and it is ironic
that a word which today applies to sexy and glamorous underwear had
such passion-dampening euphemistic beginnings. 'To wash one's dirty
linen in public', which dates back to 1895, remains an idiom today, while a
man given to adultery was known as a 'linen-lifter'. Today's borrowings
from abroad, the number of which has been steadily growing since the
watershed of the Second World War, tend to be for reasons of exoticism
and eroticism rather than prudishness. It will be interesting to watch
whether the deliberately prosaic terminology creeping into the cosmetic
market (for example **Lip Gunk**, see page 122) will in time influence our
names for underwear.

The vocabulary of underwear current in the Victorian period charts the
changes in the female shape. From the **cage crinoline** to the **cork rump**,
it was the structures beneath women's clothing which gave Victorian
fashion its form. The lacing of the bodice or corset could be so tight as to
make its wearers faint: 'Cut my lace!' was the cry of Queen Elizabeth in
Shakespeare's *Richard III*, and she was not alone. It was as a result of such
constriction that the word **straitlaced** evolved. The French philosopher
Jean-Jacques Rousseau was deeply critical of tight-lacing, remarking in
1762 that 'it is not a pleasant thing to see a woman cut in two like a wasp'.
The eventual movement away from stays, some hundred years later, went
hand in hand with the political emancipation of women.

In the mid 1970s the non-conformist designer Vivienne Westwood, who
played a central role in the emergence of punk rock, became the first
designer of the twentieth century to revive the concept of the corset in its

original form. Her use of historical garments set a new trend and was taken to represent women's new-found glamour and self-confidence. Madonna's wearing of a Jean-Paul Gaultier corset during her 1990 world tour became iconic and reconfirmed the phenomenon within fashion of underwear becoming outerwear in much the same way as the T-shirt has done, and as the bra and the branded knickers or thongs, (seen above the waistband of the new hipsters in the pattern of the so-called **whale tail**), are doing today. The corset, it seems, has come full circle, and is matched by the resurrection of some of the vocabulary of its time. **Petticoats**, **knickers**, **bustles**, and **bodices** are all freely referred to in descriptions of catwalk glamour, as the flounce of the 'maximalist' look makes a comeback.

Meanwhile another, less favourable term has also come back into fashion. **Pantywaist**, which began its life as a simple descriptor of a child's garment before becoming an insult to describe someone weak and ineffectual in the 1930s, has been a common term used in criticism by some Americans to a British audience of anti-war protesters: 'your Euro-brethren are panty waists' reads one typical online posting.

Relative newcomers on the underwear scene are **boyshorts** (or **shorties**), **tanga panties** (low in front and high in the leg, with a so-called **Brazilian cut**), **tap pants** (loose-fitting shorts, usually of silk), and **racer bras** (with straps which run between the shoulder blades).

The terms in the following timeline give an idea of both the fashion and linguistic tastes of their time, from the demure **combinations** of the 1880s to modern **scanties**. Those terms for male underwear are far more direct, including **jock** (a slang term for 'penis'), and today's self-confident **posing pouch**. The year given for each of the examples below is the date of the first citation held by the *OED*.

Body-shapers

1400 **stays**: a laced underbodice stiffened by strips of whalebone. The use of the plural is due to the fact that stays were traditionally made in two pieces glued together.

1464 **petticoat**: originally 'petty coat', or 'little coat', a tunic or chemise. It went on, in the early seventeenth century, to mean a skirt as distinguished from a bodice, worn either externally or beneath the gown or frock as part of the costume, and trimmed or ornamented; an outer, upper, or show petticoat.

1520 **farthingales**: a framework of hoops within a petticoat, worn under women's skirts to extend and shape them. The term is a corruption of the Spanish *verdugado*, from *verdugo* meaning stick or rod.

1592 **busk**: a strip of wood, whalebone, or other material, passed down the front of a corset and designed to stiffen it. The term probably comes from the French *bûche* meaning a splinter of wood.

1618 **bodice**: a sanitized version of 'bodies'. Today's **body**, which emerged in the 1980s, is a woman's all-in-one undergarment with fastenings in the gusset.

1788 **bustle**: a stuffed pad or cushion, or wire framework, worn beneath the skirt of a woman's dress. The item was also known as a 'dress-improver'.

1850 **crinolines**: stiffened or hooped petticoats. The literal meaning of crinoline is 'horse' (the French *crin*) 'hair' (*lin*): the most popular kind being made out cf horsehair and linen. Varieties of crinolines included the **cage crinoline**, which gave a domed appearance to a woman's skirt.

1911 **brassiere**: the contraction **bra** dates to the 1930s. The word originates from a seventeenth-century French term for 'bodice'. Today's versions include the **balcony bra**, **miracle bra**, and the **Wonderbra**, which came in as early as 1947.

1955 waspie (a contraction of 'wasped waist'): a woman's corset or belt designed to accentuate a slender waist.

Pants and passion killers

1567 drawers: a garment for the lower part of the body or legs, often worn by pedlars and so deemed to be of low origin. By the early 1700s it had become a term used as much by the gentility as by the working class.

1831 G-string: originally a loincloth, as worn by American Indians. In the 1930s it became associated with striptease artists, and is today shortened to 'string'.

1850 pants: originally short for 'pantaloons', the word went on in American English to mean trousers of any kind. In British English 'pants' are exclusively undergarments, the female version of which are often called **panties** (1908). The slang term 'pants', or 'pile of pants', to mean rubbish, was first used in the 1990s.

1850 bloomers: also known as **rational dress**, a form of dress for women, proposed as more sensible than that in general use, and usually denoting the use of knickerbockers in place of a skirt, especially for cycling. The term originally referred to an outer garment and was named after a Mrs Bloomer who introduced the costume of loose trousers reaching to the knee.

1870 trollies: ladies' drawers or knickers. The origin of the term is uncertain, but it may derive from the word 'trolleywags' meaning trousers. It began as schoolgirl slang but became general usage in the 1930s.

1870 BVDs (an acronym for the proprietary name Bradley, Voorhees & Day): a type of lightweight boxer shorts.

1870 knickers: short for 'knickerbockers' and originally loose-fitting and long.

1884 combinations: a single undergarment covering the body and legs.

1897 jock: another term for jockstrap. The *OED*'s first citation is from the US patent office. 'Jocks' today means jockey shorts.

1924 teddy: an undergarment combining a chemise and panties.

1926 suspender belt: the first *OED* citation is from the Army & Navy Stores catalogue: 'Suspender belts…White only…each 2/6.'

1928 scanties: a general term for underwear, or for women's short knickers. Originally a US term (an extension of 'scanty' as in small), the first citation in the *OED* is an extract from the title page of *Show Girl* magazine: 'the hottest little wench that ever shook a scanty at a tired businessman'.

1934 Y-fronts: in 1910 Coopers Inc of Kenosha, Wisconsin, introduced the X-front, also memorably known as the Kenosha Klosed Krotch undergarment. The X-front was a fiddly device with two overlapping flaps and buttons. It flopped, but Y-fronts, invented by the firm Jockey and based on the jockstrap worn by athletes, have survived. When they went on sale in 1938 they became the first ever undergarments to be displayed in a store.

1934 briefs: very short knickers. Today's briefs, ironically, are larger in size than most female underwear.

1943 passion killers: undergarments, particularly knickers, which are considered unattractive and impractical. The term was first used to describe standard service knickers issued to airwomen.

1943 smalls: formerly breeches, then underclothes. Dickens refers to 'green velvet smalls' in 1837, but it is to Noel Coward that the first use in the sense of underwear is attributed in the *OED*.

1968 boxer shorts (or **boxers**): men's loose underpants similar in shape to the shorts worn by boxers.

1975 **thong**: a garment similar to a G-string, the name of which derives ultimately from the tenth-century 'thong', denoting a narrow strip of hide or leather for use in shoes and weaponry.

1995 **chuddies**: underpants. The term is used particularly among British Asians and is thought perhaps to be an alteration of the word 'churidars' (tight trousers worn by people from the Indian subcontinent). It came into more widespread use following the catchphrase insult 'Kiss my chuddies!' from the British comedy *Goodness Gracious Me*.

Trading Terms: The New Business-Speak

20

There may be no 'I' in team, but there's a 'me' if you look hard enough.
David Brent in the TV sitcom *The Office*.

I'm looking forward to downsizing.
Retiring Archbishop of York David Hope (who is now a parish priest), March 2005.

However successful, each business needs to review its product and to refresh its image if it is to remain competitive. So it is with the language of commerce, which is one of the fastest-moving areas of neologizing.

The reach of our commercial culture is such that even abstract concepts are showing signs of being commodified. The time spent by unpaid workers such as housewives or volunteers in the pursuit of shared objectives is now called **social capital**. Tony Blair has spoken frequently of a **knowledge economy**, while business managers refer to **knowledge banks**: the pooling of staff knowledge to benefit the whole business.

The business world accommodates both well-trodden jargon and creative word play. Jargon can itself be creative. Following the linguistic model set by 'e-commerce', the number of commercial models grows almost daily: we have **m-commerce** (commercial activity conducted by means of mobile phones), **t-commerce** (transactions carried out through interactive TV); **p-commerce** (position-based commerce); **d-commerce** (digital commerce); and **v-commerce** (voice commerce involving speech recognition technology). Other terms are more playful or vivid, including some listed below.

The following selection of recent words and phrases doing the professional circuit reflect the variety of influences and effects at work.

rate tart: someone who chases the best interest rates on credit cards and other forms of credit, thereby frequently switching between deals. A related term is **stoozer**, describing someone who applies for two credit cards with a zero interest rate and who transfers the maximum borrowing amount from one card to another, where it appears as a credit: some credit card companies will allow a credit to be transferred into a savings account where it earns interest.

to be bangalored: to be laid off from a multinational company which 'outsources' some of its business functions to India. Bangalore has a reputation for being a hi-tech city.

Recently, there was an interesting term added to the English language—'to be Bangalored' meant 'loss of jobs' in the US....There is even a website www.yourjobisgoingtoindia.com

The Indian Express, 2004.

throw-weight: power or influence. A citation in the *Oxford English Dictionary* from 1982 shows the term being used to describe the weight of warheads which missiles can carry onto a target. In 2005 it is cropping up in the commercial world.

His private equity partnership....has massive throw-weight.

Fortune magazine, 2005.

homeshoring: the business practice of letting employees handle customer calls from home in preference to operating an overseas call centre. The availability of broadband connection, and the difficulties of managing remote operations, is making homeshoring (and **nearshoring**) attractive to many US companies. The term is the opposite of the earlier coinage **offshoring**.

Domestic and international carriers are cutting costs by ...offshoring and nearshoring [these facilities] outside the country's borders, and even homeshoring them into employees' residences.

Commercial Property News, 2004.

empty suit: a person in a position of authority but with no real power. The term is used as much in politics (both George W. Bush and John Kerry were described thus in the 2004 presidential contest) as in business. It is a development of 'suit', denoting a high-ranking executive in an organization seen to exercise power in an impersonal way.

boiling (or **boiled**) **frog syndrome:** having inadequate contingency plans, or being insufficiently reactive to change. This term, applied to businesses which fail to observe changes in the marketplace or in customer needs, derives from an old and unpleasant tale of scientific experimentation. Although a frog placed in hot water will leap out, one placed in cold water which is then gradually heated is said to be unable to detect the slow, incremental rise in temperature: failing to react, it boils to death. By extension, companies need to be on the lookout for subtle changes which eventually amount to a large shift in the market.

Everyone is now referring to the Bank of England's interest rate policy as 'boiled frog syndrome'. Basically the Bank of England are raising interest rates very slowly and cautiously and this is the water in the saucepan on a very low heat. We, Joe Public, are the frog.

housepricecrash.co.uk, 2005.

long-tail effect: the phrase The Long Tail was coined by Chris Anderson in a 2004 article in *Wired* magazine. Anderson's thesis is that products which individually have a low turnover can collectively make up a market share that rivals the biggest players in the market. Together they represent the long tail of the demand curve on a graph of an industry's products.

In the past few weeks, the 'long-tail effect' has dominated presentations by broadcasting executives, venture capitalists, even Google's boss Eric Schmidt.

Saturday Times magazine, 2005.

Shifting down, and back up

The 1990s and early 2000s saw a pronounced move on the part of highly paid urban professionals to leave their jobs and move to the countryside in search of a higher quality of life. The lexicon of such moves necessarily kept pace, and the **work/life balance** became a standard term. A more recent trend has been the opting back into the high-stress lifestyle—**upshifting**—at a time when confidence in the supporting economy may be shrinking.

135

mouse race: a lower-stress lifestyle which results from taking a less stressful job or from moving to a smaller community. The term is a play on 'rat race', a term which has been around since the 1950s to describe a relentless work ethic.

soul proprietor: a business person who tries to balance professional life with spiritual growth.

joy-to-stuff ratio: the time available to an individual to enjoy life rather than that spent on working hard and collecting material goods (which there is increasingly less time to enjoy).

voluntary simplicity: a lifestyle chosen so as to avoid 'conspicuous consumption'.

conspicuous austerity: a lifestyle which is carefully choreographed to reflect simple living, either by an absence of material goods or by the choice of obviously inferior ones.

upshifter: someone who rejoins the high stress of professional life having experimented with 'downshifting'.

RFID (radio frequency identification): a means of establishing identification via a wireless signal between a reader and a transponder. The method is already used in ID cards giving access to buildings, but the chips are now being used to track supermarket goods.

While the loyalty card enables supermarkets to see who is buying what, RFID means they can follow the product into people's homes.

Focus magazine, 2004.

guerrilla marketing: the use of unorthodox techniques to market products and services; 'guerrilla' implying an ambush or taking by surprise. A recent example was the use of **body advertising** by Dunkin' Donuts, who recruited volunteer college students to sport forehead tattoos of their logo at several basketball tournament games.

The body billboards are a form of 'guerrilla' marketing, according to the AAF's Hilton, who said the practice capitalizes on off-beat cultural trends to carve a niche market outside the traditional mainstream.

commercialalert.org, 2004.

to comparison-shop (US): to shop around. The term dates back to 1935, but has become high-profile today as a result of the growth in Internet shopping, which makes the process both quick and simple.

to spray and pray: to spend a large amount of money and hope that you get a return on the investment.

The usual 'spray-and-pray marketing' drains hundreds of billions of dollars in mass media exercises that reach marketing messages to a large number of 'wrong people', while only trickling in small measure to 'right people'.

The Hindu Business Line, 2004.

Euphemism: an alternative word strategy solution?

A current buzzword in business practice is the use of the term **solution**. Estate agents advertise 'total move solutions', while the disposal of rubbish can also be a 'total waste solution'. The satirical magazine *Private Eye* was even told by one reader of a company which advertised 'total barrier solutions': that is, fences.

Upping the Ante: New Findings from the *Oxford English Dictionary*

21

As the rest of the language report proves, language is constantly on the move, and it is the dictionary-makers' task to try to keep pace with developments. The gold standard for dictionaries is the *Oxford English Dictionary*. The 1990s saw the beginning of the complete first revision to be carried out on the dictionary since its original publication as the *New English Dictionary* between 1884 and 1928. Since March 2000, the fruits of this revision have been published online at quarterly intervals at *OED Online (www.oed.com)*.

The *OED* is, and always has been, a dictionary built on quotations. One of the unique features of the project from its outset was that this dictionary would not only define words, but would also illustrate their meaning and usage through the use of quotations, each representing a particular stage in that word's history. In an age before computers, this meant simply reading as widely as possible. In the late nineteenth century, the project mobilized an army of readers to search through literature and record examples of words as they were used in texts. The project today still makes extensive use of this kind of system and maintains a number of reading programmes, including some dedicated to older texts which were unavailable to the original editors of the *OED*, such as newly discovered letters and diaries. The dictionary also relies on contributions of quotations from interested members of the public.

Armed with these, and with an increasing number of electronic corpora and online databases, editors working on *OED Online* have access to a wealth of searchable information which would have dazzled their late-nineteenth-century counterparts. Thanks to such media, the revision process can frequently throw up startling discoveries of earlier examples of a word in use: known as 'antedatings'.

The role of first quotations in the *OED* is to pinpoint the time at which a word or sense can first be traced in use. Rarely will the quotations be the very first instance of a word itself: in other words, when it was coined. The past year has seen a dramatic rewrite of the history of the adjective **ophthalmic**, meaning 'of or relating to the eye'. Previously, the earliest example which the *OED* could provide for this word was from the eighteenth century, where it occurred in an encyclopedia of 1728. But using detailed research and with access to new sources, the editors have discovered an antedating of three centuries, to the Middle English period, where 'ophthalmic' appears in a medical manuscript believed to have been produced before 1425.

Not all antedatings involve technical vocabulary, of course. An everyday term which has been antedated in the course of the past year is **big hair**. The earliest example of the term now comes from the early twentieth century and the US: 'She looked at him repellently through her streaming tears. "Big hair!" she cried. "Big hair!"' (J. B. Ellis, *Lahoma*, 1913). While, out of context, the quotation might inspire sympathetic nods from anyone having experienced a **bad hair day** (a phenomenon which has been delighting us with its presence since at least 1988), the woman in question is actually reacting, somewhat badly, to the bearded and unkempt appearance of her new-found companion. The specific use of the term to refer to a bouffant hairdo, especially one which has been teased, permed, or sprayed to create volume, began to appear in the 1970s—before then it was applied to any kind of long and voluminous hair. **Power dressing** on the other hand seems, fittingly, to have come into being at the very start of the 1980s—as can be seen in the earliest quotation currently given in *OED Online*: 'Women who are into Power Dressing, that is, the right kind of well cut suit, silk shirt and discreet pump, all worn in the interests of androgyny on the job, may be happy about the entry of men's suit manufacturers into the women's suit business' (*New York Times*, 16 November 1980).

While power dressing remains grounded in the 1980s, the history of other terms has undergone a dramatic reassessment. We can now say with certainty that people have been **open-minded** for longer than previously thought. Until 2004, the *OED*'s earliest evidence for this term offered the following inspiring description: 'Open-minded, truth-seeking men' (*Foreign review and continental miscellany*, 1828), but the revised material in *OED Online* now provides the following antedating of almost a century: 'Such persons generally find it to their purpose, that all the world should be open-minded but themselves' (Samuel Richardson, *Clarissa*, 1748).

While antedatings of a hundred years or more are intrinsically dramatic, at other times an antedating which may seem very slight in terms of the number of years involved can have wider implications for the entry itself. Sometimes, finding earlier evidence of a word can uncover a sense of it which has so far gone unrecorded in the dictionary. An example of this has been found with the entry for the adjective **ornate**. Until now, the earliest quotation for this word in the *OED* was found in a manuscript believed to have been produced in around 1450. The *OED Online* revision process has thrown up an earlier quotation from a manuscript from around or before 1425: '. . . wymmen in ornate abite with schame and sobrenes enowrnande þem' ('Women should adorn themselves modestly and sensibly in seemly apparel'—*The Pauline Epistles*). If there is little difference in dating, this new citation suggests a very different sense: in fact, this is the first of a number of newly unearthed quotations which record a now obsolete use of 'ornate' to mean seemly, decorous, or dignified—a meaning which is closer to the classical Latin root *ornatus* which could indicate something 'properly' as well as 'lavishly' arrayed.

Another instance where an antedating has uncovered a sense previously unrecorded in the dictionary is the entry for the now prodigious adjective **online**. For the *OED* Second Edition (published in 1989), the earliest example of this word was from 1950, in the sense of an operation or process carried out while connected to a computer and under its direct control. When, while revising the entry, the following 24-year antedating was unearthed, it was clear that, short of having stumbled upon astonishing evidence of the existence of a 1920s internet, this quotation could not be dealing with the same sense: 'Approximately two-thirds of the coal handled by the system originated at on-line mines, and one-third was received from connections' (*Economic Geography* **2** 15, 1926). These mines are 'on-line' in the sense of being situated on the route of a railway line.

Later arrivals

Researching the quotation evidence in *OED Online* does not, of course, produce only antedatings. Sometimes the opposite happens and the team discovers later evidence of a word's existence. In dictionary parlance, these are known as 'postdatings'. Sometimes this means that a word previously believed to be obsolete turns up in contemporary usage. Postdatings can sometimes be as dramatic as the antedatings.

An example of a postdating from the material revised over the past year can be seen in the entry for the noun **overpride**, meaning excessive pride. This word was cited in the *OED* as being both rare and obsolete. From the evidence available at that time, the word appeared not to have survived the Middle English period—the last example was from 1484. It was surprising then to unearth the following quotation, raising the suspicion that rumours of the word's demise may perhaps have been premature: 'It's a helpful default habit to audit ourselves periodically for areas of rigid overpride' (*Occupational Health and Safety*, 2002). In fact, from evidence uncovered in the revision process it would seem that, although the word does appear to have died out at the end of the Middle English period, it was revived in the early nineteenth century: the first example to be found of its renewed use is from Sir Walter Scott (who was in fact responsible for bringing many archaic or obsolete words back into currency, including **raid**, **derring-do**, and **gruesome**): 'By a degree of refinement... which I afterwards heard was imputed to an overpride on the part of Jeanie MacAlpine, our landlady, the apartment was accommodated with an entrance different from that used by her biped customers' (*Rob Roy*, 1817).

Stunners and Shockers: The Art of the Headline

22

Journalism largely consists in saying 'Lord Jones Dead' to people who never knew Lord Jones was alive.

G. K. Chesterton in *The Wisdom of Father Brown*, 1926.

The classic *Mail* headline which begins 'Is this the most Evil/Depraved/ Shocking...?' can almost always be answered 'actually, no'.

Andrew Marr in *My Trade: A Short History of British Journalism*, 2004.

Sex, sensation, pets, heroism.

Former *Daily Mirror* columnist Donald Zec on what makes news.

The term 'banner headline' was coined in the US shortly before the First World War. Pithy headlines, however, were in fact appearing some years earlier, and some of their salient linguistic characteristics—forerunners of those we encounter today—were present from early on. On 23 March 1884, the front-page headline of the New York *Sun* declared an election result:

Mugwump Bradley Wins

A 'mugwump' was a Republican who refused to support the Republican presidential nominee on the grounds that he was considered untrustworthy. In its allusion to a shared cultural reference, and in its use of colloquial language, the New York *Sun*'s headline already includes some of the staples of the modern headline. It also provides an early example of the practice of piling up descriptive nouns attributively (in other words, in front of the term they describe): a powerful space-saver for the headline writer who needs to catch the reader's attention using the smallest possible number of words.

In 1966, even a serious-minded British broadsheet such as *The Observer* was employing these basic techniques in headlines such as **Police stop gangland carve-up**. The modern tabloid press, especially the British red tops and their Australian counterparts, have taken the intrinsic features of the banner headline and added what are in fact poetic effects—rhyme, alliteration, and rhythm. Most crucially, they have made puns and wordplay the common currency of their headlines. In 1990 the Sydney paper *The Picture* ran a story about a Vietnamese man who had tried to escape to Hawaii by boat: its headline announced **Ratbag reffo does a rudder** ('reffo' being Australian slang for 'refugee'.)

In this form the newspaper headline could almost be said to have developed into a form of poetry, or into an officially endorsed national graffiti. In Britain, *The Sun* in particular has supplied a series of captions to British culture for three decades. Counted among its most famous headlines are **Gotcha!** (on the sinking of the Argentinian warship the Belgrano during the Falklands conflict), **One's Bum Year** (on the Queen's 'annus horribilis'), and **Freddie Starr Ate my Hamster**. Headlines such as these take on classic status, as quotable as TV catchphrases or snatches of lyrics from pop songs. The satirical magazine *Private Eye* captioned a picture of Prince Charles and Camilla Parker Bowles after their wedding announcement as **Gotcha!**—the status of the original is such that no further reference point was needed.

On 8 February 2000, an already terrible season for the Glasgow football club, Celtic, reached a new low when they lost in the Scottish Cup to the newcomers Inverness Caledonian Thistle (or 'Caley' as they are popularly known). *The Sun* managed to sum up the match with what has a good claim to be the headline of headlines: **Super Caley Go Ballistic, Celtic Are Atrocious**. These seven words represent the

essence of the genre, a fourteen-syllable play on an invented word (even if 'supercalifragilisticexpialidocious' is in the *Oxford English Dictionary*) which exists only in the collective imagination of popular culture, used to report on a football match. Only two days after being unleashed on the British public, the headline was itself reported in the *San Francisco Chronicle*. By the end of March it had appeared in other papers in the US, New Zealand, and Canada, as well as throughout the British and Irish press. The fame of the headline far exceeds that of the match it describes (at least outside Inverness).

Another case of a much-repeated headline can usefully be compared to this story. In the early 1990s, a shortage of books in a public library in Essex was apparently reported under the headline **Book Lack in Ongar**, a punningly spooneristic take on the title of John Osborne's play *Look Back in Anger*. No one, however, seems entirely sure where this story was printed, nor even what the exact story was. Such confusion (or creativity) about the context of a story's or saying's origin is typical of urban myths, and this headline has indeed become part of a common imaginative game.

As with 'Super Caley', the 'Ongar' headline offers a better story than the event whose reporting it was supposed to headline—a claim equally true of a line in the *South Wales Echo* in March 2005 which accompanied a report that the former *Clash* guitarist Mick Jones had picked Kate Moss up from Cardiff Central train station. The headline rose far above the banality of the event: **Strolling Jones gathers Kate Moss**. By contrast, the announcement in February 2005 by the *Bristol Evening Post* of the wedding of Prince Charles and Camilla Parker Bowles, **Tetbury Man Weds**, followed an established tradition of muted reports of momentous occasions from an absurdly local perspective (Highgrove House, near Tetbury in Gloucestershire, is Charles's official private residence). **Local man dies in ship disaster** was a famous—if apocryphal—headline on the sinking of the Titanic.

A good headline is not determined by stylistic devices alone. There is a special vocabulary which headline writers draw on. Equally, newspaper headlines (though determinedly colloquial) by no means follow the ordinary rhythms of speech. *The Guardian*'s Roy Greenslade notes that 'some regular phrases have no context outside the pages of a paper, such as terror purges, rings of steel, shock verdicts, death plunges and murder bids'. Other examples of apparently exclusive headline phraseology include **sex romp** (in which the women are always **stunners**), **love rat**, and **love nest**, while three-letter words such as **axe**, **wow**, **yob**, and **bid** are just as popular.

Figurative language is another useful headline tool, allowing the headline writer to condense a wealth of associations into a single allusion. **The Goliath that Smote David** was the way in which the British *Northern Echo* announced the inquiry into the Home Secretary David Blunkett's apparent expediting of a visa for his lover's nanny, while Ken Livingstone's perceived racial slur against a Jewish reporter was reported by *The Sun* as **If Anyone's a Little Hitler, It's Red Ken**.

The following headlines give a taste of the form used to best advantage.

Judge slags tag-a-lag

Daily Star, 16 November 2004, after an independent judicial report criticized the Home Secretary's plans for 'community punishment' using electronic tagging.

Nature's Fury

Financial Express (India), 27 December 2004, the day after the Asian tsunami disaster.

Snips and Snails and Sudan 1 trails, that's what ready meals are made of

The Times, 22 February 2005, on the use of the illegal additive Sudan 1 discovered in a host of ready meals imported to Britain, and playing on the nursery rhyme 'What are little boys made of?' ('Snips and snails, And puppy dog tails, That's what little boys are made of.')

Royal Wedding Snub Sensation. Heir Rage

The Mirror, 24 February 2005, on reports that the Queen would not attend her son's registry office wedding. It was reported in the *New York Post* as **Queen to Skip Chuck Nups**.

In me arms, babe

The Sun, 4 March 2005, featuring David Beckham and his new baby, and punning on the football saying 'On me head, son'.

Stamp on the Camps

The Sun, 9 March 2005, announcing its campaign to stop 'the gipsy invasion' signalled by growing numbers of illegal 'gipsy camps' in Britain.

Death by gossip

The Independent, 23 March 2005, on the beating to death of a man by vigilantes who thought he was a paedophile.

Waiter! There's a finger in my chilli!

Independent (South Africa), 25 March 2005, on the discovery of a human finger in a bowl of chilli served by the restaurant chain Wendy's.

A load of McRap

The Guardian, 30 March 2005, on an offer by McDonald's to pay rappers between $1 and $5 for every radio play of rap songs which name-check their Big Mac burger.

Why won't he give her one?

The Sun, 11 April 2005, complaining about Prince Charles's apparent aversion to kissing Camilla in public.

Papa Ratzi

The Sun, 20 April 2005, on the election of Cardinal Joseph Ratzinger as Pope. His appointment, marked in the traditional way with white smoke from the Sistine Chapel chimney, prompted a second headline **Puff Daddy**.

The supermarket that ate Britain

The Independent, 13 April 2005, above a report on the growth of the leading British supermarket chain Tesco. The headline has distant echoes of 'Freddie Starr Ate my Hamster' (see above).

Axis of weevils cast from the mould

The Guardian, 15 April 2005, on the naming of a species of beetle after America's political triumvirate of George W. Bush, Donald Rumsfeld, and Dick Cheney (*Agathidium bushi*, *Agathidium rumsfeldi*, and *Agathidium cheneyi*). The headline plays on the US President's much-used phrase 'axis of evil' in reference to the enemies in the war against terrorism.

A Kick in the Ballots

The Sun, 6 May 2005, above a picture of a subdued Tony Blair the day after the British general election, following a sizeable reduction of the Labour government's majority.

Harry Rotter the Half-Brain Prince

Daily Star, 10 May 2005, following allegations of exam cheating by Eton College on behalf of their royal pupil.

The heart says no to the body

The Guardian, 30 May 2005, on the decision by the French electorate to reject the EU constitution.

Is that loud enough for you?

Sunday Times, 3 July 2005, on the Live 8 concert in London's Hyde Park to raise poverty awareness. The event attracted over 200,000 people.

One sweet word: London

The Guardian, 7 July 2005, after the International Olympic Committee announced London as the winning city in the bid for the 2012 Olympics.

7/7

The Times, 8 July 2005, the day after deadly terrorist attacks on London's transport system, and in clear reference to 9/11.

A hundred years earlier

Below are some of the headlines making a—rather more discreet—splash in 1905.

A Judge's Wife Cured of Pelvic Catarrh

Cambridge Jeffersonian, 26 October.

Sanitation at Panama

The Times, 20 November, on the final elimination from Panama City of yellow fever, an outbreak of which had caused panic at the start of the year.

No just cause for ready ire of John Bull

Atlanta Constitution, 24 February, referring to the report of an international commission into a skirmish between Russian and British naval ships in the North Sea.

The Rising in the Caucasus. Holy War Proclaimed, Wholesale Massacre of Armenians

The Times, 13 September, on the mass killing of Armenians by Azeri Turks fighting for supremacy.

Double lynching kept very quiet

Fort Wayne Weekly Sentinel, 27 December, alleging a cover-up of the lynching of two black men in South Carolina.

A Word a Year

23

A survey of a century's worth of new words is as surprising as it is revealing. Language has the ability to reinvent itself as circumstances require, and many of the words we consider wholly modern have in fact been resurrected from an earlier era. The following chronology selects a single word for each year in the last hundred. Not all of them bear heavy historical significance, but each captures something of the cultural vibrancy of the year in which it was coined.

1905 **peace economy**

1906 **tyrannosaurus**

1907 **Boy Scout:** 'Girl Scout' was coined in 1909.

1908 **Dow Jones:** the first mention of the term in the *Oxford English Dictionary* is from the publication *Ticker*: 'The Dow-Jones System of Averages is simply a method of calculating the average price of 20 active railroad stocks and 12 industrial stocks.' The system takes its name from the US economists C. H. Dow and E. D. Jones.

1909 **jazz**

1910 **wimmin:** 'Wimmin's a toss up,' said Uncle Pentstemon. 'Prize packets they are, and you can't tell what's in 'em till you took 'em 'ome and undone 'em. Never was a bachelor married yet that didn't buy a pig in a poke' (H. G. Wells in *The History of Mr Polly*). Here the term is simply a working-class rendition of 'women'; it has since been taken up as a slightly tongue-in-cheek feminist form which avoids the ending '-men'.

1911 flight-path

1912 rinky-dink: a worthless object. To 'give someone the rinky dink' was to swindle them.

1913 migrant labor: Congress created the Federal US Department of Labor in this year, at a time when immigration through the receiving station at Ellis Island was exceeding one million entries annually.

1914 crossword: the journalist Arthur Wynne is usually credited as the inventor of the popular word game, the first of which appeared on 21 December 1913 in the Sunday newspaper *New York World*. The puzzle was diamond-shaped and contained no internal black squares.

1915 trench fever

1916 blimp: a small non-rigid airship which originally consisted of a gasbag with the fuselage of an aeroplane slung underneath; in the First World War the name was sometimes applied to a barrage balloon.

1917 triple vaccine: a vaccine against typhoid and paratyphoid, containing three species of salmonella bacteria.

1918 D-day

1919 white collar (adjective)**:** a white collar was regarded as being characteristic of a man engaged in non-manual work.

1920 new poor

1921 quantum energy

1922 yobbo

1923 environmentalism

1924 nuclear family

1925 blind date

1926 haute cuisine

1927 national lottery

1928 boogie-woogie

1929 Wall Street Crash

1930 Intelligence Service

1931 Filofax: the proprietary name for a portable filing system in the form of a loose-leaf notebook with separate sections for appointments, notes, and addresses. Although the term is long established, it was not widely known until the 1980s.

1932 brown shirt: a Nazi, so called from the brown shirt worn as part of the uniform.

1933 supermarket

1934 supernova

1935 boondoggle: a trivial, useless, or unnecessary undertaking. To boondoggle is to engage in trifling or frivolous work.

1936 bingo

1937 spam: the proprietary name of a type of tinned meat consisting chiefly of pork. The *Oxford English Dictionary*'s first citation reads: 'The 'think-up' of the name [is] credited to Kenneth Daigneau, New York actor... Seems as if he had considered the word a good memorable trade-name for some time, had only waited for a product to attach it to.'

1938 **private eye**

1939 **tickety-boo:** in order; satisfactory.

1940 **Jim Crow:** a rooftop spotter of enemy aircraft. The term, which was coined by Winston Churchill and which seems to be unrelated to the sense denoting racial segregation, relates back to thieves' slang in which a crow is someone who keeps watch while another steals. A 'crow's nest' was also a barrel or cylindrical box fixed to the masthead of a ship as a shelter for the lookout man.

1941 **daisy-chainer:** a participant in a 'daisy chain', a group of more than two people linked together in simultaneous sexual intercourse. Daisy-chaining is said to be regaining popularity, particularly among the young.

1942 **zoot suit:** a type of man's suit of exaggerated style popular in the 1940s, characterized by a long draped jacket with padded shoulders, and high-waisted tapering trousers.

1943 **Laundromat:** the proprietary name of a brand of automatic washing machines; also, by extension, a launderette.

1944 **boot camp**

1945 **cold war:** the term was coined by George Orwell in his essay *You and the Atomic Bomb*.

1946 **Gulag:** in the former Soviet Union, the name of a department of the Soviet secret police responsible between 1934 and 1955 for the administration of corrective labour camps and prisons.

1947 **pop single**

1948 **cappuccino:** this is the date when the word was absorbed into English from the Italian. It is thought to be so called because its colour resembles that of a Capuchin monk's habit.

1949 **aromatherapy**

1950 **McCarthyism**

1951 **fast food**

1952 **spycatcher**

1953 **UFO**

1954 **double helix**

1955 **tikka:** this is the date when the word was naturalized in English. In Indian and Pakistani cookery, tikka denotes a dish of small pieces of meat or vegetable marinated in spices and cooked on a skewer.

1956 **tax-and-spend**

1957 **the Pill**

1958 **sex kitten**

1959 **Barbie**

1960 **rave** (noun)

1961 **game show**

1962 **bossa nova**

1963 **machine-washable**

1964 disco

1965 nanny state

1966 center fold

1967 sleaze

1968 Klingon: a member of a fictional humanoid alien race featuring in the US TV series *Star Trek*.

1969 moonwalk: coined in the year of the first moon landing.

1970 Third World

1971 gonzo: a word coined by Hunter S. Thompson (1937–2005) to describe a style of journalism characterized by factual distortion and exaggerated rhetorical style. It went on to mean bizarre, crazy, or far-fetched.

1972 dole queue: the noun 'dole', meaning unemployment benefit and deriving from the sense of 'doling out' money, dates back to 1919.

1973 deconstruct: to analyse and interpret a text according to the theory of the French philosopher Jacques Derrida.

1974 baby boomer

1975 refusenik: originally a Jew in the Soviet Union who was refused permission to emigrate to Israel. The term was extended in the 1980s to mean a person who refuses to obey orders.

1976 Thatcherite

1977 makeover

1978 **me generation**

1979 **nouvelle cuisine**

1980 **Reaganomics**

1981 **street cred**

1982 **Valspeak:** short for 'Valley Speak', a form of slang originating among teenage girls in the San Fernando Valley in southern California.

1983 **theme pub**

1984 **body-popping:** a style of street dancing originating in the US and popular among urban teenagers, characterized by jerky robotic movements.

1985 **Prozac**

1986 **to multitask**

1987 **smiley:** a smiley face, which began as a humorous convention in email.

1988 **vogueing:** a style of dancing which imitates the characteristic poses struck by a model on a catwalk.

1989 **luvvly jubbly:** excellent, 'great stuff'. The term was coined by John Sullivan in his BBC television series *Only Fools and Horses* as a characteristic expression of Derek 'Del Boy' Trotter, a Peckham market trader. It is a reference to 'lubbly Jubbly', a 1950s advertising slogan for Jubbly, an orange-flavoured frozen drink.

1990 **smackdown:** chiefly in the US, a beating, humiliation, decisive setback, or defeat; also a bitter contest or rivalry. The term was later popularized by the US professional wrestling television show *WWF Smackdown!*.

1991 hotdesking: the practice of allocating or using desks or workstations on an ad-hoc basis rather than assigning them permanently to particular individuals, operated as a means of saving office space and resources.

1992 poptastic

1993 fashionista

1994 dotcom

1995 ladette

1996 alcopop

1997 blamestorming

1998 text message

1999 ASBO (antisocial behaviour order): a court order obtainable by local councils in Britain.

2000 speed dating

2001 war on terror

2002 SARS (severe acute respiratory syndrome)

2003 freedom fries: an alternative term for 'French fries', chosen by some Americans as a critique of the French protest against the invasion of Iraq.

2004 podcasting: making available a digital recording of a radio broadcast or similar programme on the Internet for downloading to a personal audio player.

2005 su doku

su doku

The logic puzzle 'su doku' (also written as Sudoku and Su-doku, with variations on capitalization) arrived relatively quietly in Britain when it was introduced by *The Times* in 2004. In the early summer of 2005, however, it provided an excellent example of how a new phenomenon can dramatically explode onto the scene, bringing its linguistic expression with it.

Su in Japanese means 'number', while *doku* means 'single' (literally 'unmarried'). It is believed to have originated in New York rather than Japan, where it was first called a 'number place puzzle' by Dell Magazines. Whatever its geographical origin, some scientists are likening the puzzle to a 'meme' in its behaviour: they view it as a kind of 'mental virus' which spreads rapidly.

To solve a su doku puzzle, every digit from 1 to 9 must appear just once in each of nine vertical columns, each of nine horizontal rows, and each of nine 3 by 3 boxes. In May 2005 the puzzle suddenly took off as a new and addictive phenomenon, advertised on the masthead of almost every British newspaper in a bid to outdo its rivals with more difficult or more authentic su dokus (among them the inevitably named *Sun Doku*).

Dubbed the Rubik's cube of the twenty-first century, the su doku offers a near-perfect example of how a word is propagated.

Index

Oxford English Dictionaries

Oxford Dictionary of English

Professional, College, Office, Home

- Over 355,000 words, phrases, and definitions
- The most comprehensive single-volume dictionary available

0-19-861057-2

Concise Oxford English Dictionary

Professional, College, Office, Home

- Over 240,000 words, phrases, and definitions
- The best-selling concise dictionary: authoritative and comprehensive coverage

0-19-860864-0
0-19-861010-6
(thumb-index edition)

Compact Oxford English Dictionary of Current English

Office, Home, School

- 145,000 words, phrases, and definitions
- Now in colour, with extra help on writing good English

0-19-861022-X

Pocket Oxford English Dictionary

Home, School

- 120,000 words, phrases, and definitions
- Extra help with usage, grammar, and spelling

0-19-861029-7

Select a dictionary to suit your needs ...

Paperback Oxford English Dictionary

Office, Home, Family reference

- 120,000 words, phrases, and definitions
- Dictionary definitions and 4,700 entries for people and places

0-19-860454-8

Little Oxford English Dictionary

Office, Home, Family reference

- 90,000 words, phrases, and definitions
- Extra help with punctuation, grammar, and word formation

0-19-860452-1

Colour Oxford English Dictionary

Home, School

- 90,000 words, phrases, and definitions
- Clear, two-colour text with easy-to-follow guidance on grammar and spelling

0-19-860569-2

Oxford English Minidictionary

Office, School, Travel

- 90,000 words, phrases, and definitions
- All-purpose minidictionary: portable and durable

0-19-860865-9

Oxford English Thesauruses

Oxford Thesaurus of English

Professional, College, Office, Home

- 600,000 alternative and opposite words
- The most comprehensive single-volume thesaurus of English available

0-19-860862-4

Concise Oxford Thesaurus

Professional, College, Office, Word games

- 365,000 alternative and opposite words
- Authoritative and comprehensive coverage plus extra noun lists

0-19-860453-X

Oxford Compact Thesaurus

Office, School, Home

- 300,000 alternative and opposite words
- Now in colour, with extra help on improving your writing skills

0-19-861030-0

Oxford Paperback Thesaurus

Home, Family reference, Word games

- 325,000 alternative and opposite words
- Thousands of example sentences

0-19-860371-1

Enrich your vocabulary and increase your wordpower...

Little Oxford Thesaurus

Home, Office, Family reference

- 140,000 alternative and opposite words
- Vocabulary supplement to increase your wordpower

0-19-860461-0

Colour Oxford Thesaurus

Home, School, Family reference, Word games

- 140,000 alternative and opposite words
- Robust and portable, with a two-colour text and lots of examples for easy usage

0-19-860449-1

Oxford Mini Thesaurus

Office, School, Travel, Word games

- 140,000 alternative and opposite words
- All-purpose mini thesaurus: portable and durable

0-19-860711-3